THE PENGUIN POETS

THE PENGUIN BOOK OF FIRST
WORLD WAR POETRY

Jon Silkin was born in London in 1930, and educated at
Wycliffe and Dulwich Colleges. In 1947 he spent a year
working as a journalist, which was followed by eighteen
months national service in the army as a teacher in the
Education Corps. After leaving the army he worked as
a manual labourer in London for six years, followed by
two years of teaching English to foreign students in a
language school. During these years Jon Silkin
established his reputation as a poet. Thereafter he held
the Gregory Fellowship in Poetry at the University of
Leeds (1958-60), and in 1965 moved to Newcastle where
he co-edits the literary magazine *Stand*. In recent years
Jon Silkin has visited America several times, giving
poetry reading tours, and has taught at the famous
Writers' Workshop at the University of Iowa. His
volumes of poetry include *The Peaceable Kingdom* (1954),
Nature with Man (1965), which was awarded the Geoffrey
Faber Memorial Prize, *The Principle of Water* (1974) and
The Little Time-keeper (1976). He has also published
Out of Battle, a critical study of the poetry of the First
World War.

THE PENGUIN BOOK OF
FIRST WORLD WAR POETRY

EDITED AND WITH AN INTRODUCTION BY
JON SILKIN

PENGUIN BOOKS

Penguin Books Ltd, Harmondsworth,
Middlesex, England
Penguin Books, 625 Madison Avenue,
New York, New York 10022, U.S.A.
Penguin Books Australia Ltd, Ringwood,
Victoria, Australia
Penguin Books Canada Ltd, 2801 John Street,
Markham, Ontario, Canada L3R 1B4
Penguin Books (N.Z.) Ltd, 182–190 Wairau Road,
Auckland 10, New Zealand

First published 1979
Published simultaneously by Allen Lane
Reprinted 1979, 1980

Made and printed in Great Britain by
Richard Clay (The Chaucer Press) Ltd,
Bungay, Suffolk
Set in Monotype Ehrhardt

CONTENTS

Contents

ACKNOWLEDGEMENTS

We are indebted to the copyright holders for permission to reprint certain poems:

Apollinaire: to Christopher Middleton for 'Shadow';

Arcos: to Christopher Middleton for 'The Dead';

Blunden: to A. D. Peters & Co. Ltd and Harcourt Brace Jovanovich, Inc. for 'Two Voices', 'Preparations for Victory', 'Come on, My Lucky Lads', 'The Zonnebeke Road', 'Vlamertinghe: Passing the Château, July, 1917', 'Third Ypres', 'Gouzeaucourt: The Deceitful Calm', 'La Quinque Rue', 'The Ancre at Hamel: Afterwards' from *Undertones of War*; to A. D. Peters & Co. Ltd for '1916 seen from 1921', 'Report on Experience', 'The Midnight Skaters';

Cummings: to MacGibbon & Kee Ltd/Granada Publishing Ltd and Harcourt Brace Jovanovich, Inc. for 'my sweet old etcetera' from *Complete Poems*;

Ehrenstein: to Christopher Middleton for 'The Poet and War';

Ford: to The Bodley Head and The Estate of Ford Madox Ford for 'That Exploit of Yours'; to The Bodley Head, The Estate of Ford Madox Ford and Mrs Theodora Zavin for an extract from 'Antwerp';

Goll: to Patrick Bridgwater for 'Recitative (I)' and 'Recitative (VIII)';

Gurney: to Chatto & Windus and The Literary Estate of Ivor Gurney for 'The Silent One' from *Poems of Ivor Gurney 1890–1937*; to The Literary Estate of Ivor Gurney for 'To His Love', 'The Bohemians', 'War Books', 'Strange Hells';

Heym: to Patrick Bridgwater for 'War' and Christopher Middleton for 'Why do you visit me, white moths, so often?';

Jones: to Faber & Faber Ltd for an extract from *In Parenthesis*;

Kipling: to The National Trust, Eyre Methuen Ltd, the Executors of the Estate of Mrs George Bambridge and Doubleday & Co. Ltd for 'Epitaphs of the War' and 'Gethsemane';

Klemm: to Albert Langen Georg Müller Verlag and Patrick Bridgwater for 'Clearing-Station';

Lawrence: to Laurence Pollinger Ltd, The Estate of the late Mrs Frieda Lawrence and The Viking Press for 'Song of a Man Who Has Come Through';

Lichtenstein: to Patrick Bridgwater for 'Leaving for the Front';

Manning: to John Murray (Publishers) Ltd for 'Grotesque' from *Eidola*;

Monro: to Gerald Duckworth and Co. Ltd for 'Carrion' from 'Youth in Arms' from *Collected Poems*;

Read: to Faber & Faber Ltd and Horizon Press (New York) for 'The Happy Warrior', 'The End of a War' and 'A Short Poem for Armistice Day' from *Collected Poems*;

Rickword: to Carcanet New Press Ltd for 'The Soldier Addresses his Body' and 'Winter Warfare' from *Behind the Eyes: Collected Poems and Selected Translations*;

Rosenberg: to Chatto & Windus Ltd, The Literary Estate of Isaac Rosenberg and Schocken Books Inc. for 'August 1914' from *Collected Poems*;

Sassoon: to Mr G. T. Sassoon and The Viking Press for 'A Working Party', 'The rank stench of those bodies haunts me still', 'The Death-Bed', 'Prelude: The Troops', 'Counter-Attack', 'Base Details', 'Lamentations', 'Does It Matter?', 'Glory of Women', 'Repression of War Experience';

Schnack: to Christopher Middleton for 'Nocturnal Landscape';

Stramm: to Patrick Bridgwater for 'Guard Duty'; to Michael Hamburger and Carcanet Press for 'Battlefield';

Thomas: to Mrs Myfanwy Thomas and Faber & Faber Ltd for 'A Private', 'Man and Dog', 'The Owl', 'In Memoriam (Easter, 1915)', 'Fifty Faggots', 'This is No Case of Petty Right or Wrong', 'Rain', 'Roads', 'February Afternoon', 'The Cherry Trees', 'As the Team's Head-Brass', 'Gone, Gone Again';

Trakl: to Michael Hamburger and Carcanet Press for 'Lament' and 'Grodek';

Ungaretti: to Jonathan Griffin, Jon Silkin and Arnoldo Mondadori Editore for 'Vigil', 'Brothers', 'Rivers' and 'No More Crying Out';

Vildrac: to Christopher Middleton for 'Relief'.

We are also indebted to Jon Stallworthy and John Bell for permission to reproduce the British Museum manuscript of 'Strange Meeting' by Wilfred Owen.

Every effort has been made to trace copyright holders. The publishers would be interested to hear from any copyright holders not here acknowledged.

INTRODUCTION

Reconciliation

Word over all, beautiful as the sky,
Beautiful that war and all its deeds of carnage must in time be
    utterly lost,
That the hands of the sisters Death and Night incessantly
    softly wash again, and ever again, this soil'd world;
For my enemy is dead, a man divine as myself is dead,
I look where he lies white-faced and still in the coffin – I draw
    near,
Bend down and touch lightly with my lips the white face in
    the coffin.

                – From *Drum Taps*, Walt Whitman

STANDING IN THE WAY

I

Even compassion must now be circumspect, for if it doesn't try to do away with, or limit, the war that causes the suffering, it's indulgent. At best compassion like this walks behind the system.

Our humanity must never be outwitted by systems, and this is why we are at our most vital when our intelligence is in full and active cooperation with feeling. We shall never not be political again, and the best way to be this, among other things, is to think *and* feel; and if this co-operative impulse is permeated with values we can decently share, we stand a chance, as a species, of surviving. For that, I think, is what is at stake.

In this sense, the war poets owe much to the early politics of Wordsworth and Coleridge; although Burns and Blake preceded them, Wordsworth and Coleridge were at the beginning of a consciously political ethos and felt themselves as individuals enmeshed in politics. Coleridge must have felt this strongly for him to have exclaimed, in a letter, even as early as 1796:

I have snapped my squeaking baby-trumpet of sedition.

Wordsworth never attempted to invalidate the generosity or humanity of his earlier politics; but he spent his more conservative years, say from 1800 on, in modifying those views, framing them in perspectives which imply coolness, deliberation, judgement and, finally, a rejection of the political structures that had claimed generosity and humanity as their essential distinguishing characteristics.

In a sense this is too rapid, for a sketch is needed of the problems that confront any evaluation of the First War poetry. We are too close and too distant from the experience the poems struggle so balefully with. Too close, in the sense that it is our problem still, and recognizably our kind of warfare; too distant in that we can, and often do, treat that war as our history. Yet the language of that war is still very much ours; the value system inhering in the language of those poets remains the basis of our value system. The pretensions and disclaimers have changed, somewhat, but not the way in which the preoccupations are evaluated. This fairly immerses one in the problem because both the theme and its language are touched on in this description. And the problem can be perceived, very simply, if we say that the value we attach to the theme and any apprehension of it, is not necessarily the same as the value we attach to an expression of it. Yet the degree to which we feel a discrepancy exists between an evocation of the theme and its crystallization in, say, the superb coming together of Rosenberg's 'Dead Man's Dump' is an expression of the difference and the disjunction between art and life. The disjunction is disturbing. It sometimes makes us ashamed, as though we had betrayed the theme (and those caught up in it) for the sake of the poetry. Owen didn't solve the problem with 'The Poetry is in the Pity', he merely identified it. For to absolve the poet of the necessity of making good poetry by concealing that problem in the pity (not that I'm suggesting Owen did this) is only second to absolving the poet of his or her need for pity by letting him be content with his 'craft'. That last word can have unpleasant connotations; it carries much of the self-approbating superiority that Eliot's 'practitioner' bears, and which Leavis censures.[1] It carries the sterility of uninvolved distancing. There may be a case *for* the poet distancing him or herself (not as considerable a one as Eliot, and others, have suggested) but surely the case to be made is not that such distancing ought to be done, but that it may, sometimes, be tried; the tension that that puts a poet under as he grapples with the diverse impulsions of experience, response and creation, is what's desirable, not the easily achievable and self-approving male ideal of disinterested contemplation. I am most interested not in self-validation, but the need to feel rather than see clearly. Here the Imagists have not served us so well.

I tried to present the claims the various critical positions made upon our attention in *Out of Battle*; here is one of them: '[the] preoccupations [of those who lived through the First World War] are also ours, so that in searching for a satisfactory critical approach one is tempted to examine

[1] See F.R. Leavis, *Thought, Words and Creativity*, chapter 1.

their work as history, reducing poems to documents that might yield solutions to our problems.' I made this point (one sees) in order to suggest how undesirable such a solution was for a (satisfactory) reading of the poems, let alone as an answer to the problem of war. But on re-consideration, were we ever given the chance to erase war by using the poets' apprehensions, we'd be foolish not to take that chance. The question scarcely bears considera-tion; of course one would sacrifice the poetry to the pity and the compunction, if what were achieved by that were peace for ever. For if the poet's message can be used effectively, then used it should be. The question however involves a consideration as to whether the reduction of poetry to case-book exhortation is truly the most effective mode of persuasion, the winning of deep, authentic assent. I don't believe it is, and my reasons for saying this are, after all, simple. Human beings are not composed of mind, or cerebration, or even intelligence; they are not even, as a rule, composed of the extremities of good and evil, although twentieth-century experience might persuade one otherwise. Since we are composite, the most successful breach of the human mind is made in composite fashion. Samuel Johnson recognized this when he advised that the business of the poets was to reach through to the reader's *senses*. This de-emphasizing of intelligence, at a time when it might be supposed it was the prime attribute, supposed so on account of the ethos as well as the particu-lar critic, suggests how strongly the intelligence, when it is working fully, recognizes the limitations of its mode. Johnson's insight dazzles one with its modesty, a quality that he was, after all, ambiguously gifted with. He is so sure he is right, but the surety in this instance comes not from intellectual arrogance but from a perception of what can be shared; it's of the same order as his insight regard-ing the common reader: 'I rejoice to concur with the common reader [concerning Gray's 'Elegy']; for by the common sense of readers uncorrupted with literary prejudices, after all the refinements of subtilty and the dogmatism of learning, must be finally decided all claim to poetical honours.' And surely Johnson is right. Intellectual capacities and colourations differ. The surface of anything is more susceptible to quick, discernible change. We think or don't think the same ideas; that doesn't seem to matter so much as whether we don't feel similarly. It is a mercy that we do share some fairly large areas of feeling. If that were not the case we would have perished. Our survival, after all, depends not on our productivity but upon our agreement that a certain amount of productivity, in certain areas, is essential – not for our well-being – we aren't *entitled* to that – but for our survival. We don't have the right, for that matter, to survival; but put on that footing, we can at least make our own way in this matter and not trust to providence, which has shown itself tricky. What we do not seem able to do is agree on how we shall survive, and how do it with full regard for life.

We come on this word life again, and it is a religious as well as a political question.[1] It can't at any rate be answered by suitable fiscal arrangements for the next ten years' oil-flow or some such. Nor for that matter can it be solved in simple ethnic harmony. We shall perish of thinness of soul if all we can agree on is whether circumcision and pigmentation are desirable or at least 'permissible' physical characteristics or attributes. The co-existence we sporadically believe desirable results from a conjunction of thought and feeling. The quickness of the quick bird does not deceive the eye. The inhumanity of human beings kills humanity. That it kills much else besides does not occur to us because we are not so attuned; but as soon as we are concerned with how we shall survive together, we can be sure that we will see ourselves as an ingredient of the whole,

[1] See Leavis, op. cit.

rather than as 'the proper [and only] study of mankind'. These are after all some of the considerations of what is, arguably, Owen's best, certainly one of his most profound, poems – 'Exposure' ('For hours the innocent mice rejoice'). The density of image and complexity of syntax attest the almost overwhelming crux, and Owen's response to it ('how shall our best values be best defended'). That he was ever able to interrelate successfully these diverse elements into a poem is a major achievement – the kind of achievement that comes when the writer has accumulated more experience than literary confidence and habit; when the pressure of experience and feeling and idea is so great that one hardly knows the poem is getting written. This to be sure is exaggeration; we know that Owen worked and re-worked this poem. Even so, the work fuses so many ideas and feelings that I can't think of any other poem of his in which the desire to answer the questions he raises is as strong. Had we only this poem of Owen's we would have had to have given him major if incomplete status as a poet.

I want to return to the question of de-centralizing man's concern with himself, and I want to repeat the suggestion that this, and the question of what we find valuable, are religious questions (portentous though this may sound). At the same time I should like to suggest that the pre-occupations of the two undeniably, possibly four, major war poets, Rosenberg, Owen, and perhaps David Jones and Herbert Read, were, whatever else, religious.

This raises a number of extremely delicate questions that have, of course, been dealt with – no, not dealt with but attempted – before. I can't now begin a sketch of the problem in its principal manifestations, but I can touch on the problem as it involves dogmatism. And after all, if one is sure one is right, what accommodation can there be for another point of view? Only the demonstration of one's error by another. Such a problem was probably one reason for Coleridge (and after him, Eliot) formulating the idea of suspension of disbelief, or belief. In Coleridge's case it was done, perhaps, for the purposes of accommodating in his poetry an expression of those supernatural forces which did not consort with Christianity. With Eliot, and how have the times changed, it is a question of how he can accommodate non-Christian readers in dialogue with a professedly Christian poetry. (Interested readers will note that I ascribe, correctly, a capital letter to the words Christ, Christian and Christianity; whereas it took Eliot something over forty years before the Jew in 'Gerontion' (1919) could be graced with a capital letter. Eliot is fortunate in that there is no rancour in heaven.)

The problem may be seen more easily after this small digression. Eliot could hardly bring himself to give the 'Jew' a capital letter, so great was his distaste for Jews. It can't therefore be supposed that it's easy for anyone with strong beliefs or feelings to grant the justice of another viewpoint.

'Thus you see how pure Christianity will not fit in with pure patriotism,' Owen tells his mother in a letter dated [16?] May 1917.[1] The problem isn't much different, and it's intractable. If you believe something is wrong you cannot, out of tolerance, or any other mode, convince yourself that it's right. We aren't dealing here with logic, for belief operates in that area of human feeling where thinking has cooperated with it to produce assent (or dissent). For Owen, killing was wrong.

'And am I not myself a conscientious objector with a very seared conscience?' he wrote in the same letter.

This is the nub of Owen's poetry, from which the compassion flows. Compassion is the blood that issues from the wound, and the wound is caused by our soldiering. In 'Strange Meeting' the compassion, significantly, is

[1] Wilfred Owen, *Letters*, p. 461.

reserved, not for the soldiers of his own side, but for the enemy he has killed. And there cannot be two ways about this. You may kill for pay; or because you are told to; you can enlist because other poets (like Ezra Pound) believe it best for you (see below, pp. 31–2); you may do it in order to survive. You may do it out of hatred, or from blood-lust. But the motives do not change the nature of the act.[1] And if you set it like this, your poetry will have a moral centre and integrity that is incontrovertible. This kind of strength, with a supple poet, is of infinite use, but it raises reciprocal problems. For readers like John H. Johnston, who believe in the categorical imperatives of duty (the duty to serve, in this instance) those who do not directly engage this nexus of obligation do not accord with his schemata; he is therefore able to down-grade most of the poets who dissent and who therefore (apparently) employ the 'lyric' mode of poetry, a mode totally unfitted it seems for adducing the experience of war in any real way. With this circular argument he remorselessly chastises most of the poets to whom this book is devoted, except for David Jones (about whom he wrote an earlier essay)[2] and Herbert Read; and these poets fit his thesis in as much as they write a poetry remotely describable as 'epic'. The integrity of his position is only, curiously enough, more

---

[1] In the introduction to his anthology *Men Who March Away*, Ian Parsons notes Shakespeare's *3 Henry VI* (II, v, lines 73–5 and 121–2):

> [*Enter a son that hath killed his father, bringing in the dead body*]
> HENRY:　O piteous spectacle! O bloody times!
> 　　　　　Whiles lions war, and battle for their dens,
> 　　　　　Poor harmless lambs abide their enmity . . .
>
> [*Enter a father, bearing his son*] . . .
> FATHER:　I'll bear thee hence, and let them fight that will,
> 　　　　　For I have murdered where I should not kill.

The apprehension is summed up in the last line of the quotation.

[2] 'The Heroic Vision', *Review of Politics*, 24 January 1968.

inflexible than Owen's; but then duty is more inflexible, though not necessarily stronger than, compassion.

'The theme is indeed important,' exclaims Wordsworth in his *Preface* to the second edition of *Lyrical Ballads* (1800).[1] The theme is important not only because it's palpable, but because of the nature of its substance.

Can we imagine a poetry embodying our convictions, which we would not respect? There are certainly three responses to that question, and they might occur in the following order:

1. No; these are my convictions.
2. Yes, I can; a crude representation of my attitudes distorts my beliefs.
3. However, it does not follow that I will like all the poetry that is written in a sensibility I find acceptable either. But it does mean that the mode of expression is a part of the theme.

Given these stages of understanding, I believe it's possible to evaluate the war poets for their explicit ideas. It is also equally possible to evaluate the sensuous re-enactment with which their themes are fleshed. I'll therefore attempt two kinds of scheme. The first will be an arrangement, or progression, of poets according to a developing consciousness, in relation to the war and the "good" of society as a whole. (As Jones suggests in his *Preface* to *In Parenthesis*, war is a different kind of peace.) The second scheme will consist of an attempt to group poets in terms of sensibility and language.

2

Trail all your pikes, dispirit every drum,
March in a slow procession from afar,

---

[1] Consider the resemblances of basic attitudes between Wordsworth's and Owen's *Prefaces*.

Ye silent, ye dejected men of war!
Be still the hautboys, and the flute be dumb!
Display no more, in vain, the lofty banner.
For see! where on the bier before ye lies
The pale, the fall'n, th'untimely sacrifice
To your mistaken shrine, to your false idol Honour.

     –'The Soldier's Death', Anne, Countess of Winchilsea

   Surely this is an archetypal anti-war poem. Christopher
Logue, it's true, has given us his version of the Patroclus
episode from Homer; and Simone Weil in her brilliant
and moving essay 'The *Iliad*, or the Poem of Force' has
shown us how, in a sense, Homer has pre-empted all later
objections to war.[1] Yet much as I would agree with all
that Weil so admirably asserts, there is much else in
Homer besides objections to war. Indeed one might regard
Homer as a prototypical twentieth-century poet because of
his ability to juxtapose opposed sets of ideas (according to
Jowett, 'The unity of opposites was the crux of ancient
thinkers in the age of Plato'). Certainly this juxtaposing
adduces problem-making as the principal mode of human
thought, where before there were either random pieces of
thought which were occasionally seen to be contradictory,
or else, simple erasure of contradictions. We try not to
behave like that now. Man is no longer the simple em-
bodiment of belief; his mode of existence is to be in
opposition to himself; Yeats tells us that we make poetry
out of the argument with ourselves. It may be. Yet in terms
of war, in terms, that is, of the current *total* view of war,
Homer is not modern, and Winchilsea is. She approximates
the two themes of spurious honour, and the sacrifice of
youth, in so unflinching a way that we do not ask the literary,
over-literary, questions, when and by whom. In a letter to
Miss Seaton of 1915 Rosenberg wrote: 'Why do you ask me
who wrote it [a poem about London]? "Truth should have

---

[1] *The Wind and the Rain.*

no man's name." [1] Yet, after all, the *when* is interesting
because it serves to remind us of two (conflicting) percep-
tions. First, that the poets of the First War were not the
first to write against war in a consistent achieved way. And
second, that even so there was no continuous tradition, or
any tradition as such, of anti-war poetry from which these
First War poets could draw sustenance. To which one
might add the fact that there was hardly any anti-war
poetry (apart from George Gascoigne's 'The Fruits of
War', Thomas Campbell's 'Hohenlinden' and Southey's
'The Battle of Blenheim') if we discount the Romantics,
and Blake. And that's it: Wordsworth and Coleridge wrote
highly politicized apprehensions of war. It's true that
Coleridge's objections to war, insensitivity to which is
incarnated in the *civilian*, are brilliantly achieved in 'Fears
in Solitude' (1798). But as Basil Willey suggests in his
Coleridge biography, having made the unanswerable
objections to war, Coleridge proceeds to answer them.
Here are two passages from the poem which fairly rep-
resent both aspects of the crux:

> Thankless too for peace . . .
> Secure from actual warfare, we have loved
> To swell the war-whoop, passionate for war!
> Alas! for ages ignorant of all
> Its ghastlier workings . . .
> We, this whole people, have been clamorous
> For war and bloodshed; animating sports,
> The which we pay for as a thing to talk of,
> Spectators and not combatants! No guess
> Anticipative of a wrong unfelt . . .
> We send our mandates for the certain death
> Of thousands and ten thousands! Boys and girls
> And women, that would groan to see a child
> Pull off an insect's leg, all read of war,

[1] *Collected Works*, p. 346.

The best amusement for our morning-meal!
The poor wretch, who has learnt his only prayers
From curses, who knows scarcely words enough
To ask a blessing from his Heavenly Father,
Becomes a fluent phraseman, absolute
And technical in victories and defeats,
And all our dainty terms for fratricide;
Terms which we trundle smoothly o'er our tongues
Like mere abstractions, empty sounds to which
We join no feeling and attach no form!
As if the soldier died without a wound;
As if the fibres of this godlike frame
Were gored without a pang; as if the wretch,
Who fell in battle, doing bloody deeds,
Passed off to Heaven, translated and not killed;
As though he had no wife to pine for him,
No God to judge him! Therefore, evil days
Are coming on us, O my countrymen!
And what if all-avenging Providence,
Strong and retributive, should make us know
The meaning of our words . . .

And then, twelve lines later:

Stand forth! be men! repel an impious foe,
Impious and false, a light yet cruel race,
Who laugh away all virtue, mingling mirth
With deeds of murder; and still promising
Freedom, themselves too sensual to be free
Poison life's amities, and cheat the heart
Of faith and quiet hope, and all that soothes
And all that lifts the spirit! Stand we forth;
Render them back upon the insulted ocean,
And let them toss as idly on its waves
As the vile sea-weed, which some mountain-blast
Swept from our shores!

And then, as though it weren't enough to present this
contra-picture of the crux, Coleridge will even qualify his
patriot qualifications:

> And oh! may we return
> Not with a drunken triumph, but with fear,
> Repenting of the wrongs with which we stung
> So fierce a foe to frenzy.

I myself don't believe Coleridge is presenting both sides, in that balanced way Willey suggests, so much as he is responding to two pressures: those of his political ideals and those of patriotism (in the modern sense). Even so Coleridge anticipates nearly all those objections to war that the 1914–18 poets were to pursue.

Wordsworth was more truculent and more dour on the question. His position was not so much pacifist as political; he and his Republican friend Beaupuy chance to meet

> a hunger-bitten girl,
> Who crept along fitting her languid gait
> Unto a heifer's motion, by a cord
> Tied to her arm, and picking thus from the lane
> Its sustenance, while the girl with pallid hands
> Was busy knitting in a heartless mood
> Of solitude, and at the sight my friend
> In agitation said, ''Tis against *that*
> That we are fighting,' I with him believed
> That a benignant spirit was abroad
> Which might not be withstood, that poverty
> Abject as this would in a little time
> Be found no more, that we should see the earth
> Unthwarted in her wish to recompense
> The meek, the lowly, patient child of toil,
> All institutes for ever blotted out
> That legalized exclusion, empty pomp
> Abolished, sensual state and cruel power,
> Whether by edict of the one or few;
> And finally, as sum and crown of all,
> Should see the people having a strong hand
> In framing their own laws; whence better days
> To all mankind.
>
> – *The Prelude*, IX, 510–32

Byron recollects all the insouciant arrogance of the civilian who defuses the death of the soldier in a line of compensatory print:

He fell, immortal in a bulletin.

– *Don Juan*, canto VII, xx

And in *Don Juan* (finished 1822), Byron anticipates the distinction between the front-line soldier and the 'at base' officer, which Sassoon makes in 'Base Details':

Also the General Markow, Brigadier,
    Insisting on removal of the *prince*
Amidst some groaning thousands dying near, –
    All common fellows, who might writhe and wince,
And shriek for water into a deaf ear, –
    The General Markow, who could thus evince
His sympathy for rank, by the same token,
To teach him greater, had his own leg broken.

– *Don Juan*, canto VIII, xi

As Byron anticipates Sassoon, so Shelley does Owen's 'Strange Meeting' (for that matter, so does Whitman with:

For my enemy is dead, a man divine as myself is dead

in 'Reconciliation'). Here is the relevant passage from Shelley's *Revolt of Islam* (1818):

'Soldiers, our brethren and our friends are slain.
    Ye murdered them, I think, as they did sleep!
Alas, what have ye done? the slightest pain
    Which ye might suffer, there were eyes to weep,
    But ye have quenched them – there were smiles to steep
Your hearts in balm, but they are lost in woe;
    And those whom love did set his watch to keep
    Around your tents, truth's freedom to bestow,
Ye stabbed as they did sleep – but they forgive ye now.

'Oh wherefore should ill ever flow from ill,
    And pain still keener pain for ever breed?

We all are brethren – even the slaves who kill
   For hire, are men; and to avenge misdeed
On the misdoer, doth but Misery feed . . .

When I awoke, I lay mid friends and foes,
   And earnest countenances on me shed
The light of questioning looks, whilst one did close
My wound with balmiest herbs, and soothed me to repose;

And one whose spear had pierced me, leaned beside,
   With quivering lips and humid eyes; – and all
Seemed like some brothers on a journey wide
   Gone forth, whom now strange meeting did befall
   In a strange land, round one whom they might call
Their friend, their chief, their father, for assay
   Of peril, which had saved them from the thrall
Of death, now suffering. Thus the vast array
Of those fraternal bands were reconciled that day.'

               – canto V, x–xiii

I hope I have sufficiently suggested how much, how
typically, as well as how individually, each of the Romantic
poets, with the interesting exception of Keats, anticipates
in his poetry the positions of the First War poets. All that
was lacking was the actual experience! And this, either
of combat, or the times. For that matter, were the Napol-
eonic wars so different in the misery they produced?[1]

The only surprising thing is that the questions the
Romantic poets raised so profoundly should have been so
profoundly forgotten by the onset of the First War. That,
at least, is the impression one gets from the average per-
formance of those poets who typify the first stages of
response to the war. And these may be fairly represented
by Brooke in whom, as Geoffrey Matthews observes, we
have a poet who embodies the patriot aspirations of the
ruling class. And in a sense, dare one suggest it, he
represents not only the ruling-class aspirations but also –

---

[1] Consider Hardy's *The Dynasts*.

although the tone is wrong – the working-class patriot as well, for whom the war was either a release from the constraints of drudgery, or, and it was almost the same thing, an apparently extended vacation. Vacation it certainly was, but not in the way in which one understands it here, but rather the evacuation of compunction, responsibility and understanding. All that civilization had painfully built by way of mercy and restraint was dropped, if the cheering, smiling crowds photographed in Berlin and London are any guide. Of this, Brooke is also fairly representative – his mode is after all different – although, as Geoffrey Matthews again notes: 'the five famous "war sonnets" . . . are not war poems at all, except in the most accidental sense, but – to put it crudely – poems celebrating the export of English goods'.[1]

Here are the opening lines of Brooke's 'The Soldier':

If I should die, think only this of me:
    That there's some corner of a foreign field
That is for ever England. There shall be
    In that rich earth a richer dust concealed;
A dust whom England bore, shaped, made aware . . .

This is as candidly imperialist as Kipling, even if it is, less frankly, an inferior copy of Hardy's 'Drummer Hodge':

Yet portion of that unknown plain
    Will Hodge for ever be;
His homely Northern breast and brain
    Grow to some Southern tree,
And strange-eyed constellations reign
    His stars eternally.

We have thus in Brooke the first of four stages of consciousness which might be set out thus:

1. Not so much a stage in consciousness as a passive reflection of, or conduit for, the prevailing patriot ideas,

and the cant that's contingent on most social abstract
impulses. Brooke fairly offers a version of this as do
Sassoon's earliest war poems, which are, indeed, Brooke-
like in character.

2. The second stage of consciousness is properly
represented by Sassoon. In part, its character is com-
prehended by Joseph Cohen's description of what Sassoon
fulfils in 'the role of the angry prophet'.[1] But this doesn't
do full justice to the strengths (and weaknesses) of
Sassoon's position. He protests against the war variously:
through the recreation of physical horror (he describes
himself as a 'visually submissive' poet); through anger
and satire; and through sardonic distancing. Whatever
means he uses, he more than adequately represents a
frontal protest 'against the political errors and insincerities
for which the fighting men are being sacrificed'.[2] To adapt
Disraeli's concept of 'the two nations', if one nation is
comprised of all the soldiers, the other is made up of all
the civilians of the fighting nations. It is the 'callous
complacency' of the civilian Sassoon wishes to penetrate.

3. The next stage in consciousness is that of compassion.
In some ways, to typify Owen as the poet of compassion
is to distort his achievement and endorse a weakness in
the poetry. Nevertheless what distinguishes Owen, and
his sensuousness, from Sassoon, and his, is compassion –
strength of feeling. His is not the more intimate response
of pity and tenderness, for Owen's compassion is fairly
often olympian and thus, inevitably perhaps, paternalistic.
I don't mean by this that it isn't authentic. Owen must
appear as one of the most authentic voices of compassion
in English poetry; and one would also want to include in
that claim the Scottish poet Henryson's *Testament of*

---

[1] Joseph Cohen, 'The Three Roles of Siegfried Sassoon', *Tulane
Studies of English*, VI, 1956.
[2] *The Complete Memoirs of George Sherston*, p. 496.

Cresseid; for Cresseid, too, is a victim of war. Even so, the more intimate, singular range of pity is achieved more by Rosenberg than Owen; the wonder is that Sassoon achieves neither compassion nor pity. Hardly, at any rate. That must seem a desperate assertion, but a close inspection of the war poems will, I think, bear out the truth of this. The reasons for this lack are perhaps that, given the limited energy in any individual, most of Sassoon's is poured into a recreation of physical horror, and the concomitant responses of anger, disgust, and the mode of satire. Engaged with these preoccupations, and most readers would, I think, agree that they are his principal ones, there's not much available energy remaining. Moreover Sassoon's own clue to his (poetic) personality is strongly suggested in the phrase 'visually submissive' poet. Sassoon's moral indignation found anger its most conducive mode; and although one might infer from his anger against civilian complacency that he felt compassion for the soldier, it isn't usually explicit. It's therefore fair to suggest that in as much as the third stage of consciousness, compassion, may be fairly represented as an advance on the second (anger), Owen represents that third stage in a way that Sassoon rarely does. It's however equally true to say that Owen learned the mode of anger, satire, and concision, from Sassoon if anybody. The earlier, four-line stanza version of 'The Dead-Beat' (which I prefer) is as much in the mode of Sassoon as anything might be; and profits from being so. The incisiveness of 'Smile, Smile, Smile', a late poem (September 1918), has the muscle and sharpness of Sassoon's best war poetry. Moreover the crucial point with Owen is that the compassion works best when it is in active cooperation with his anger or satire, as it is in, for instance, 'Insensibility'. This, with 'Strange Meeting' and 'Exposure', is surely one of his best poems. The danger with Owen's compassion is that it can tend to self-indulgence, and perhaps even attempt to assuage the guilt of the killer. Additionally, it may, in its most unguarded moments, be manipulated by war-mongers. Nothing in the combination of anger and compassion will work that way:

But cursed are dullards whom no cannon stuns,
That they should be as stones.
Wretched are they, and mean
With paucity that never was simplicity.
By choice they made themselves immune
To pity and whatever moans in man . . .

4. This leads directly into the fourth and last stage of consciousness, where the anger and compassion are merged, with extreme intelligence, into an active desire for change, a change that will re-align the elements of human society in such a way as to make it more creative and fruit-ful. What such active life may consist of, and how it works, may be understood from the closing lines of Rosenberg's playlet *Moses*:

I'd shape one impulse through the contraries
Of vain ambitious men, selfish and callous,
And frail life-drifters, reticent, delicate.
Litheness thread bulk; a nation's harmony . . . .
So grandly fashion these rude elements
Into some newer nature, a consciousness
Like naked light seizing the all-eyed soul . . .

The nature of this energy in its wholly unrancorous but fully adult character may also, typically, be seen in his other unfinished play, 'The Amulet/Unicorn' fragments; although the word fragment suggests far less than what was actually achieved. Energy is very much the key term; energy creates the harmony of music which is beyond, but inclusive of, its desire for beauty. That is the story, and it's within such a compass that Rosenberg's 'war poetry' fits. The care with which such a conception of energy must be handled may be readily imagined; but that

Rosenberg achieves this care in consummate fashion may be seen, best seen perhaps, in this brief quotation from 'Dead Man's Dump':

A man's brains splattered on
A stretcher-bearer's face;
His shook shoulders slipped their load,
But when they bent to look again
The drowning soul was sunk too deep
For human tenderness.

The tenderness of that passage is beyond Owen's habitual reach and it comes, not just from a ready identification with the victim, which characterization it is only, in some ways, too easy to make for Rosenberg; it comes from the energy of the generosity, but it arrives also with that scrupulous care with which Rosenberg attends not to the victims, but a victim, the one man on the battlefield that Rosenberg sees at that time, in that place. He may acquire representative status, and no doubt does; but that isn't Rosenberg's ambitious concern as it is, I think, Owen's. If this seems unfair to Owen, I refer the reader to the two versions of Owen's most famous line – in 'Strange Meeting';[1] I quote them in the order in which they were written, and note that, of course, the second version erases the first:

I was a German conscript, and your friend

and

I am the enemy you killed, my friend.

It may be that the final version is more effective; it is certainly more generalized, and for that reason attains, perhaps, the condition of universality. But it pays for that by losing the intimacy and specificity of the first, which Owen must surely have recognized, for his poetry con-

[1] See below, pp. 58–69, 'Owen's Metrics and his Compassion'.

stantly oscillates between a Sassoon-like specificity and universality. For Rosenberg this was not a problem. Indeed, for him, it cannot be said that there was a problem; the victim's presence was such that no conversion of the specific to the universal was either possible or necessary. The victim's condition was such that the necessary octane drove the mind to recreate an evaluation in the most austere and intimate terms. Rosenberg does not appear to write out of recollection (indeed, as a private soldier, he got much less leave during which he might have "recollected" than the officer Owen).[1] Owen's tendency was to recollect; presumably the opportunities of leave merely confirmed his preference for perspective and synopsis. 'It seemed that out of battle . . .' I shall want to say more about Rosenberg's language, and not only in comparison with Owen's, but this isn't the point at which I'm likely to make my best case. Yet it's worth mentioning here that the complexity of Rosenberg's concerns is matched with a richness of imagery and rhythm – movement overall – which is sensuously more *alert*, I think, than Owen's. Ever so slightly, Owen's language suffers from the settled quality of the "spokesman". For whom, and, for that matter, to whom (at that time) was Rosenberg speaking? The audience is clearly in his mind, but it's not one he could easily have found. Certainly not an audience composed of readers such as Pound, as Rosenberg's unfinished letter (December 1915) to this correspondent suggests:

Dear Mr Pound
Thank you very much for sending my things to America. As to your suggestion about the army I think the world

---

[1] To be fair, Owen was approximately sixteen months absent from the Front. Suffering shell-shock, he arrived at Craiglockhart War Hospital in June 1917. Sassoon arrived in the August. Owen was, voluntarily, back at the Front by September 1918, and dead by 4 November 1918.

has been terribly damaged by certain poets (in fact any poet) being sacrificed in this stupid business. There is certainly a strong temptation to join when you are making no money.[1]

What Pound actually thought about Rosenberg[2] (apart from Pound's apparent suggestion that Rosenberg enlist – which he did, somewhere at the close of October 1915) is contained in this letter to the editor of *Poetry*,[3] Harriet Monroe: 'He has something in him, horribly rough but then "Stepney, East" . . . we ought to have a real burglar . . . *ma che*!!!' (The irony of the little Italian phrase, this early in Pound's life, is resonant.)

While we are with Pound and his role of impresario with regard to Rosenberg, it might be instructive to compare this famous passage concerning war, in Pound's 'E.P. Ode pour L'Élection de son Sépulchre' (1920) with a part of a not well-known poem by Rosenberg. The latter ascription of 'not well-known' to this poem by Rosenberg is something of a tautology in that there is hardly, if at all, a poem of Rosenberg that is well-known. Not that such a condition is the be-and-end-all, but it comes as something between profound irritation and disappointment that the more abstract, altogether thinner, passage from Pound should have received the overwhelming attention it has when it appears to be so removed from an apprehension of what war entails on a generation of participants. As with Owen's second version of the line from 'Strange Meeting' (above), what it gains in deftness – not that *Owen* is deft – it loses in the comparison with the less easily manipulable but experiential density of Rosenbergian imagery; that I do not exaggerate will, I hope, appear from a comparison

[1] *The Complete Works of Isaac Rosenberg*, p. 346.
[2] Quoted in *Isaac Rosenberg: Poet and Painter*, p. 104.
[3] *Poetry* published Rosenberg's 'Break of Day in the Trenches' and 'Marching' in vol. IX, 3, December 1916.

of, and, in the end, a contrast between, these two passages.
Firstly Pound's:

came home, home to a lie,
home to many deceits . . .
usury age-old and age-thick
and liars in public places . . .[1]

hysterias, trench confessions . . . .

There died a myriad,
And of the best, among them,
For an old bitch gone in the teeth,
For a botched civilization,

Charm, smiling at the good mouth,
Quick eyes gone under earth's lid. . .

and, from Rosenberg's 'August 1914':

What in our lives is burnt
In the fire of this? . . .

The gold, the honey gone –
Left is the hard and cold.

Iron are our lives
Molten right through our youth.
A burnt space through ripe fields
A fair mouth's broken tooth.

One notes that Rosenberg in one respect shows Pound to

---

[1] Of the 'pro patria/usury' passage Leavis writes in *New Bearings
in English Poetry*, (p. 110):
   – That is a dangerous note, and only the completest integrity
   and the surest touch could safely venture it. But we have no
   uneasiness. The poet has realized the war with the completely adult
   (and very uncommon) awareness that makes it possible to nurse
   indignation and horror.
   I am unsure of this judgement. Pound's view is, as I've tried to
suggest, too synoptic, too abstract an 'experience' – if indeed it is
that – of the war. And what war is it, precisely, that he did experi-
ence? Not Rosenberg's, or Owen's – of that we may be sure.

disadvantage. For where Pound in the stanza beginning 'There died a myriad' contrasts the best of them (the dead soldiers) with the worst of It (the decaying civilization), no such neat, and to my mind, simplified, contrast occurs in Rosenberg's lines. If Rosenberg's characterization of 'Youth' is perhaps a bit too pious in 'ripe fields', it is also a mouth that has broken teeth, broken not, as Pound would imply in his lines, by a decadent civilization that gets its youth to do its fighting for it, but, as Rosenberg implies, by the youth (as well) even though they are conscripted by their elders. In Pound, the civilization is botched even more by those who ought to know better and who are about to consign their youth to destruction; in Rosenberg, youth will do the killing and take on their part in the destruction. It's the same thrust that is made in 'Break of Day in the Trenches'. It's no good, that is, hiding the actions of murder behind pity; only by showing forth the actions clearly do we stand a chance of understanding them, and changing ourselves. As Hardy characterized it (speaking of his meliorist position, in effect), change 'exacts a full look at the worst'.

I'd like to revert to a suggestion I made regarding a crucial feature of this fourth stage of consciousness, of which Rosenberg is the ample representative. I mean a comprehensiveness; and this, I think, is achieved by the open-mindedness which is so typical of Rosenberg's strength. As Denys Harding wrote:[1] '[he] brought language to bear on the incipient thought at an earlier stage of its development. Instead of the emerging idea being racked slightly so as to fit a more familiar approximation of itself, and words found for *that*, Rosenberg let it manipulate words almost from the beginning, often without insisting on the controls of logic and intelligibility.' The strength and the comprehensiveness both can be seen to be con-

---

[1] *Experience into Words*, p. 99.

scious attributes of Rosenberg's character – the noun takes up both meanings here – in this quotation from a letter to Laurence Binyon of 1916: 'I am determined that this war, with all its powers for devastation, shall not master my poeting; that is, if I am lucky enough to come through all right. I will not leave a corner of my consciousness covered up, but saturate myself with the strange and extraordinary new conditions of this life, and it will all refine itself into poetry later on.'[1]

3

These four stages of consciousness outlined above offer one way of considering the differing work in relation to the one theme, of war. The structure provides a means of assigning value to the poets' work as they evaluate the experience of war. But we are also to consider their relationship, not merely to the theme, but also to each other, as they explore their experience through the emotional, sensuous and intelligent aspects of their individual languages.

In considering their relationships to each other, we can refer back to the prototype bond (and contrast) between Wordsworth and Coleridge as they explore their attitudes to France and War. In some such way we could consider the differences between Rosenberg and Owen. We may of course evaluate their poetry as a construct confined within the English language; but what gets squeezed in there is the supposed synonymity between language and sensibility. English sensibility is not the prerequisite for *good* English poetry, or for good poetry written in English; and I suggest that were this accepted the estimation of Rosenberg's poetry would be higher.

Rosenberg's poetry – all poetry – is made of response and

[1] *Complete Works*, p. 373.

evaluation, and with the poetry of war, response will be strong, provoking active insistent evaluation of the civilization. But although the evaluations are affected by the culture (here, the language) they aren't wholly determined by it. Blood isn't English, nor is pain. But the language will help to shape the evaluations; it is part of the culture that has nurtured the writer. Even so, we might consider the similarities of Imagism, Expressionism and even Acmeism, where such simultaneities suggest not cultural singularity but extra-national homogeneity. Yet within such a tendency towards homogeneity, or perhaps running beside it, is, of course, the tendency towards cultural particularity. Something is said to be typically English, or Russian. That we use this linguistic formulation points, however, to a weakness in the perspective, since the whole concentration of particularity tends to be dispersed by generalized notions of 'typically'. Yet that the phrase is not wholly unjust may be seen in that in many ways the English that Rosenberg employs is not the English of Owen, Read, Sassoon, or yet Jones. Whether it is better or worse is not quite the question here; it is more to do with the sense that English may have plural rather than singular standards. Rosenberg's language, at any rate, is exploratory; his poetry seeks to re-shape culture by introducing new ideas and alignments, and one might say that this aspiration is most apparent in Rosenberg's language. In his brief, moving note to Rosenberg's *Complete Works* (1937) Sassoon spoke of how Rosenberg '*modelled* words with fierce energy' (how opposite in conception to Sassoon's own modest apprehension of himself as a 'visually submissive' poet). Neither apprehension is unjust, but it might be better to stress that Rosenberg's *energies* were fierce; it is at this deeper level of response that we begin with Rosenberg, for one might also suggest that the newness and richness of Rosenberg's language comes from these energies and their seeking to reshape a culture. In that sense Rosenberg's language is the only possible one for his aspiring energies.

The notion of judging poetry as poetry – which involves the suspension of disbelief – may act as a good corrective for those readers and critics who care for literature only as a source of ideas. But that reaction, and it is one, now disingenuously renounces substance in verse as though what the poetry were saying was only of distant concern. Yet if words have lexical value we must attend to these. We can't properly escape their meaning, though we may evade them in an effort, as Eliot did, to insist more fully on their rhythmic and tonal value (or even the concentrated bud of feeling – image or dark embryo – with which I'm more in sympathy); but we may also disregard the meanings because it is intellectually, morally and emotionally easier to do so. In this instance, sensibility is the last refuge of the aesthete.

Neither extremity of consideration, of language or of message, is satisfactory, and perhaps the simplest expression of my dissatisfaction can be suggested by my sense of how each approach, on its own, violates the poem, which then becomes either a message or a word machine. Yet it's clear we can obtain some understanding of war through an examination of the language and sensibility of war poetry.

It's easy to suggest such an examination, difficult to execute it. Should we consider the non-combatant F. S. Flint's poem 'Lament', or Sorley's Owenesque 'When you see millions of the mouthless dead'? What kinds of apprehensions are obtained by comparing Hardy's prophetic 'Channel Firing' with Owen's first war poem 'Exposure' (the first poem of war which he *began*); what happens to the comparison when one introduces Rosenberg's 'Dead Man's Dump'? The size of the task is off-putting, and the kind of justice that considers one poem per poet anthologized here isn't of any use. We need some kind of conscious system not only to promote insight into the differing languages each poet uses, but also to reveal the limitations of the inquiry. In a sense, that last is the most important point, for a limitation should be seen to exist in relation to an inquiry concerning the language each poet uses. Not but that we aren't aware, gropingly, of the limitations of positivism. When we think of pain it isn't through language; it is via our memory of the experience.

The problem of the war poets is one of bringing one's present if changing consciousness to bear upon 'man's inhumanity to man'. No doubt Wordsworth and Coleridge were aware of this, feelingly so; but how does one think about it, and bring one's feeling, sensibility and intelligence into cooperative balance? For the problem is to do with consciousness as well as sensibility. Burns's phrase 'man's inhumanity to man' (adapted by Wordsworth) expresses sensibility; the tone approximates a feelingly moral stance set in a metronomic (that Wordsworth reproduces) in which every syllable registers. It is a way of obtaining every colouration from the words as they profess a "mere" idea. And when Coleridge speaks of the newspaper report of casualties in war as being

The best amusement for our morning-meal

we respond to the tone of his moral certainty, as much as we do to what Basil Willey points to as Coleridge's 'and what if' syndrome.

Moral indignation is sufficient to associate two poets, and when their consciousness, or focus, settles on the same areas of concern, there is, you might think, no seeing them apart. This twinning, however, doesn't quite occur, and this is to do with the different energy levels. It could be said that Wordsworth's energy runs risks in forming its own habit of activity, even when there's little for it to say; whereas with Coleridge, the sensibility is finer. But as

Coleridge knew with all the pain of his nature, the care runs to dejection, and the energy-loss to entropy (= a state of dead equilibrium). This astonishing prototype of association by similarity which, however, shows forth the strongest possible contrast, might serve as a model for a consideration of the war poets and their sensibilities. Perhaps I shouldn't let the attribute of sensibility stand as the sole consideration as far as these poets are concerned, but it will do for the moment because it provides a means of relating the like/unlike pair of Wordsworth and Coleridge with at least one of the groupings of war poets I now want to make. Sensibility is, as it were, the umbilicus of our understanding whose genesis is with Wordsworth and Coleridge. This grouping could, if one wished, be replicated for we might bring into this prototyping the Byron/Shelley/Keats constellation; since there is nothing in the war poets that does not in some way, some crucially important way, go back to these poets also. For instance, Owen owes as much to Shelley, in the end, as he owed at first to Keats; 'Strange Meeting', 'The Show', and 'Arms and the Boy' will testify to this (consider the *Revolt of Islam*, canto v, stanzas ix–xiii; *The Triumph of Life*; *The Mask of Anarchy*). And Sassoon owes much more to the Byron of *Don Juan*, cantos vii and viii than he does to – Masefield. Yet crucial in a different way, Wordsworth and Coleridge do not set the communal, social experience of England aside in quite the way that Byron and Shelley do, or are forced to do; so that the two former poets stand as the great originators of social disaffection in the face of war and political allegiance.[1]

As far as the First War poets are concerned then, I suggest (below) the following groupings. And such groupings cross the apparently divided impulsions (divided and separate) of moral injunction and passion. I say

---

[1] Although Blake anticipated much of their earlier politics.

'apparently' for under what head would compassion come?
It's undoubtedly moral in intention, yet we wouldn't deny
it gives pleasure, if not to the recipient, then certainly to
the giver. And it's appropriate here to look at that strange
paradox which may be characterized by suggesting that
the recreation of others' pain, in art, gives pleasure as it's
apprehended with compassion. It would be simple if the
diagram were a representation of that reciprocal process
whereby the inevitable pain we suffer is sometimes
alleviated, to an extent, by others' sympathy; and that
when we witness this in art, our apprehensiveness on
account of our own misery is lessened, although not dis-
persed. If that was all there were to it, we should not
puzzle over the matter further, but in fact the relations
between suffering, and the re-transmission of it, *in art*, are
more complex. Yeats's formula, which he took from
Arnold, that 'passive suffering is not a theme for poetry',[1]
begs so many questions, and rides roughshod over them,
that I think it best not to argue with it; except to question
the notion that all suffering is passive, and that a recreation
of that suffering in art is mere passive "activity".[2]

A more profitable, patient, and altogether more fully
adult and intelligent approach, as Yeats's certainly isn't, is
found in Shelley's *The Triumph of Life*:

---

[1] *The Oxford Book of Modern Verse.*
[2] In the *Preface* to his *Poems*, 1853, p. 3, Arnold wrote:

> What then are the situations, from the representation of which,
> though accurate, no poetical enjoyment can be derived? They are
> those in which the suffering finds no vent in action; in which a
> continuous state of mental distress is prolonged, unrelieved by
> incident, hope, or resistance; in which there is everything to be
> endured, nothing to be done. In such situations there is inevitably
> something morbid, in the description of them something monot-
> onous. When they occur in actual life, they are painful, not tragic;
> the representation of them in poetry is painful also.

This accounts for his withdrawing of *Empedocles on Etna*. It was
restored by Arnold in 1867.

See the great bards of elder time, who quelled

The passions which they sung, as by their strain
May well be known: their living melody
Tempers its own contagion to the vein

Of those who are infected with it – I
Have suffered what I wrote, or viler pain!
And so my words have seeds of misery.

–lines 274–80.

The argument is so complex that I can follow it best by
paraphrasing its various stages. The bards subdued their
pain (and their apprehension of it in others) by the re-
creation of it in their poetry. This is a primary laying-out
of the idea as a paradox whose cohesion depends on the
apparent contradiction of not wanting pain and the
"imaginative" recreation of it (pain, or any other strong
passion, when recreated in art is conquered). The next
unit is to do with the living melody, which is not only
poetry but a recreation in poetry of suffering; it's a proto-
type of 'the Poetry is in the pity'. Suffering isn't only an
essential ingredient of certain kinds of poetry, such poetry
couldn't exist without it. Shelley, however, isn't interested
in classical ideas of catharsis, as the fine ending (which
Rosenberg admired) of *The Cenci* shows; here, of course, he
wants to inculcate indignation at those social forms which
entail suffering, and in this he's at one with the war poets.
These are complex arguments, but what I think Shelley is
saying is that not only can this poetry not be made without
an apprehension of others' suffering, but also that such an
apprehension, *recreated in poetry*, tempers the poet's own
suffering ('contagion'). We are all, in any case, similarly
'infected'. So the suffering and pain are unavoidable. This
in its turn gives rise to a poetry of suffering which itself
tempers suffering. Yet the paradox here is that although
the poetry may 'temper' the suffering, it does not 'evacuate'
it. So far from doing this, the poetry contains the 'seeds

of [future] misery'. Thus the poetry serves both to temper misery and to bring an apprehension of it to those who know neither others' pain nor yet their own. There is in this poetry something so profoundly *real* that I find myself questioning the idea of catharsis. And this is because I think, as the war poets did, that we must not dispel others' suffering, but, on the contrary, absorb it. 'Seeds' is particularly fine because it not only promises the growth of a feeling apprehension of misery but the burgeoning of the human being who does this. This is not of course the only apprehension of life, but it is a crucial part of it; without this, pleasure becomes *mere* pleasure (consider Keats in this confirmation), hedonist and thin. Which Keats certainly is not. Moreover pleasure alone leaves unexplored, and unexplained, a part of life before which, if we do not look at it, we retire baffled, with a sense of not having begun to live. This is as true for those who believe that misery is the only mode; but then I'm not advocating this, and nor was Shelley.

Despite the apparently exclusive concentration on suffering in the only poetry of Owen that's worth consideration, we do feel, in the presence of this poetry, a similar paradox. If we say that Owen enjoys suffering, this gives a wrong valuation of his work although it might, occasionally, be correct. If we say that we enjoy his apprehension of others' suffering, that identifies in us a masochism, or callousness, we do not necessarily have. But this at least puts us in possession of Shelley's 'temper the contagion'; it is Owen's way. If we share another's suffering deeply, the enjoyment as such lies, I believe, in the transmission of sympathy. But that is only a part of the experience of Owen's poetry because we get a profound enjoyment, and satisfaction, from the concomitant transmission of, not only another's apprehension of suffering, but also of the artefact in all its parallel evaluative deliberation and shape. We are moulded (perhaps permanently changed somewhat) by an experience of the poem's movement, its sensuous transmission in a particular crystallization. The joy, if we aren't envious, is in another's achievement which operates on us with its own life. That operation produces in us a reciprocating pleasure.

Pleasure, as referred to in the immediately preceding lines, is a considerable part of Owen's poetry (I take for granted the reader's agreement that the *other* major constituent is Owen's moral passion); and this pleasure is in mutual operation between poet and reader. Owen's Keatsean sensuousness promotes this, and the sensuousness may be seen in Owen's determination to obtain maximum sensuous fulness for both the horrific and the peaceable. Compare for instance (the rather Shelleyean) 'The Show' with the Hyperion-like opening of 'Strange Meeting'. For although both are about the war, one is totally absorbed in the horror; the other, by implication, strives towards peaceable harmony, even though it pessimistically concludes that the condition is unlikely to be achieved. Thus:

And Death fell with me, like a deepening moan.
And He, picking a manner of worm, which half had hid
Its bruises in the earth, but crawled no further,
Showed me its feet, the feet of many men,
And the fresh-severed head of it, my head.

– 'The Show'

and

It seemed that out of battle I escaped
Down some profound dull tunnel, long since scooped
Through granites which titanic wars had groined.
Yet also there encumbered sleepers groaned. . .

– 'Strange Meeting'

In identifying one of Owen's central modes as enjoyment, sensuous enjoyment, it shouldn't escape our notice that this is counter-weighted by his at times censorious, certainly didactic, morality. This is all right; the opposition of modes is usually good for poetry, if the poet is sufficiently robust. But this conjunction of sensuousness and morality associates Owen with Sassoon, who has a similar conjunction of attributes. With Sassoon, however, the proportion of attributes, or their emphases, is reversed. Owen doesn't allow his censoriousness or didactic impulse to dominate his sensuous life. With Sassoon it does dominate, and perhaps this informs us as to why his strongest mode is that of satire and anger; it also offers us an insight as to why Sassoon should see himself as a 'visually submissive' poet. He tends, that is, to photograph the horror, and then become morally outraged; as a rule he doesn't *sensuously* enact his evaluating responses. In his 'Moles' fragment of 1817 Coleridge enacts a very different mode:

> – They shrink in, as Moles
> (Nature's mute monks, live mandrakes of the ground)
> Creep back from Light – then listen for its sound; –
> See but to dread, and dread they know not why –
> The natural alien of their negative eye.[1]

Coleridge is able, in lieu of his being able to feel, to fall back and draw upon what I should call the inner sensuousness, that is, to employ his metaphysical mode. Byron, in

[1] In fact Coleridge's mode owes much to those lines critics often adduce (*qua* Leavis) as evidence that Pope's imaginative core was lit by metaphysical poetry:

> Most souls, 'tis true, but peep out once an age,
> Dull sullen pris'ners in the body's cage:
> Dim lights of life, that burn a length of years
> Useless, unseen, as lamps in sepulchres;
> Like Eastern Kings a lazy state they keep,
> And close confin'd to their own palace, sleep.

> – 'Elegy to the Memory of an Unfortunate Lady'

Coleridge concentrates the metaphysical paradox.

The Two Foscari, is able to operate a similar power, and this enables him to compensate (as I understand it) for his want of feeling imagination:

> 'Tis said that our Venetian crystal has
> Such pure antipathy to poisons as
> To burst, if aught of venom touches it.
> You bore this goblet, and it is not broken.
>
> – V, i.

Although this attribute is much less a regular part of his composition than it is Coleridge's. And one should say that not only does Sassoon lack the sensuous power that Coleridge only intermittently, however powerfully, employs, but that, like Byron, the metaphysical imagination is (even more) rarely available to him. (It's significant that Sassoon turns to Byron's satire as the exemplar of what is to become his strongest mode – it is, we conclude now, Byron's strongest mode as well; certainly the one in which he operated so well with such frequency).

Sassoon's morality then is strong to the point of overtaking his sensuousness. The tension that exists in Owen between morality and sensuousness doesn't exist in Sassoon because the former is so much stronger. This can best be seen by comparing the expression of 'Base Details' with, say, the sensuous horror of 'Counter-Attack':

> The place was rotten with dead; green clumsy legs
> High-booted, sprawled and grovelled along the saps
> And trunks, face downward, in the sucking mud,
> Wallowed like trodden sand-bags loosely filled;
> And naked sodden buttocks, mats of hair,
> Bulged, clotted heads slept in the plastering slime.

But the sensuous horror of this contrasts not only with the wrathful execution of 'Base Details' but also with the sub-Keatsean/sub-Shelleyean pastoral of 'The Last Meeting'. This latter in any case suffers *further* depreciation from a comparison with its ancestor 'Adonais':

He is made one with Nature: there is heard
His voice in all her music, from the moan
Of thunder, to the song of night's sweet bird.

As Shelley immortalizes Keats by merging him with nature
(thus personifying him in something like the way Keats
personifies Autumn), so Sassoon does with his friend:

Ah! but there was no need to call his name.
He was beside me now, as swift as light.
I knew him crushed to earth in scentless flowers,
And lifted in the rapture of dark pines.

Yet there are several crucial differences between Shelley
and Sassoon in these passages; one is that while Sassoon
"robs" nature to immortalize his friend (thus lending an air
of doubtfulness to the whole procedure), Shelley is as much
concerned with the processes of immortal nature as he is
with Keats. He thus sets up just the right kind of tension
between the immortality of nature and the diffusion of
Keats's spirit (by virtue of Keats's practice as a poet)
within nature; which is perhaps the best one can do for
anyone after their death. The essential point is not to lose
sight of *nature*'s activity; otherwise nature will merely
seem to suffer an unreal use of its facilities for the purpose
of promoting one's friend's memory. This, surely, is the
abuse Sassoon practises. But there is another problem
here, to do with the failure, in 'The Last Meeting', of
sensuous power; and it can be put by suggesting how
Sassoon's sensuous energy divides; one part tending, as
Middleton Murray observed, to photographic power, the
other towards "bloodless" pastoralism. Even in Sassoon's
'Repression of War Experience', where the maximum of
horrific sensuousness, obtainable in the moths' bumping
against the light, is possible, the recreation there isn't as
delicate and powerful as Owen would have made it. This
can be checked by placing the work (in its entirety) beside
Owen's corresponding "post-war" poem 'Disabled'.

In fact Sassoon's strengths are quite other. What he does is to fill the traditional forms of iambic rhymed pentameter, then generally associated with some form of pastoral "indulgence", with the horrific matter of war, thereby jolting his readers' expectations doubly, once with the matter itself, and again with the matter within the expectations of a particular form. These shock-tactics of juxtaposition can be seen in essence in the phrase 'glum heroes' (from 'Base Details') where the traditional patriotic cant of hero is undermined by the realist everyday truthful word 'glum'. Who rejoices marching to his death?

Yet the grouping of Sassoon with Owen is meaningful. They share a version of realism, a concreteness and specificity, in confronting the horror of trench combat; and they share in a condemnation of civilian callousness and unregenerate ignorance. It was because these possibilities for specific expression lay, however undeveloped, in Owen that Sassoon was able to influence him in this, Sassoon's, most powerful mode. So to this extent the two poets overlap; each contributes in a mode taught by the older man, but in which the younger isn't deficient (see for instance 'Smile, Smile, Smile'). Where they don't overlap is in what is Owen's particular strength, his sensuous compassion, and in Sassoon's deficiency, a slack pastoralism (that has little genuine sensuousness in it). Sassoon's energy-level does not run in Owen's direction.

At this point, we may begin to see which poet, at his most typical, synthesizes some of Owen's sensuousness with something of Sassoon's profile, something of the incisive prose virtues which Sassoon deploys in bringing home his messages. One might locate a collocation of these attributes in Edward Thomas, in, for instance, 'As the Team's Head-Brass':

> Every time the horses turned
Instead of treading me down, the ploughman leaned
Upon the handles to say or ask a word,

About the weather, next about the war.
Scraping the share he faced towards the wood,
And screwed along the furrow till the brass flashed
Once more.

Leavis's account of Thomas[1] that the 'outward scene is
accessory to an inner theatre . . . . the end of the poem
['October'] is not description', has hardly been bettered;
but the account doesn't settle with this other part of
Thomas's work which is fairly represented by the poem
above, and which is characterized by the inward connec-
tion with the outward concern. A considerable amount of
Thomas's 'war poetry' (he who never wrote a poem once
he reached the trenches – never had the chance) can be
taken under this description, and it is moving in that it
shows how Thomas does not sacrifice his apprehension of
the outer world for the sake of dramatizing the inner (his).

In adverting to Thomas's imaginative power, of which
that kind of selflessness is a fair example, one is brought
to face Isaac Rosenberg's imagination, which outstrips, in
a fully purposeful way, all the other poets of that war.
With that assertion to view one might consider, in a kind
of Wordsworthian/Coleridgean opposition, the two prin-
cipal nexes of power, Owen and Rosenberg, since it's out
of such a comparison that we'll obtain a fuller view of them
and the other war poets.

One might begin in taking up Welland's hint that Owen
is a bridge between the nineteenth and twentieth centuries
by suggesting that he's a traditional poet.[2] I mean that
he's content, in the main, to use the verse forms and leave
them much as he found them. That is why the innovation
of half-rhyme stands out and is made much of. This is not
entirely fair. The (deliberate) ambiguity of sex and death
moves beyond Swinburne's pleasure/pain nexus in being

[1] *New Bearings in English Poetry*, p. 55.
[2] *Wilfred Owen: A Critical Study.*

over-seen by moral judgement. Consider parts of 'Greater Love'. But in the main the energies Owen deploys are traditional as far as form and language are concerned. What is new, newer than anything Eliot and Pound achieved, is the close apprehension, emotionally speaking, of combat. Owen's energies are those of indignation and compassion and these are to do with the substance, the experience, he recreates and evaluates. And yet, although not denying Rosenberg the value of his experiential substance, it would be right to say that he brought a powerful, interpretative sensuous language to bear on the realities of war (and hence society). In his sensuousness, he, too, contrasts with Sassoon; and this sensuousness, used to indicate the desirable social re-alignments, can be seen in *The Amulet/Unicorn* fragments. In a different way, this societal aspiration can be seen in 'Daughters of War' and 'Dead Man's Dump'. So a comparison between aspects of Owen's 'Strange Meeting' and 'Insensibility' with some in Rosenberg's 'Dead Man's Dump' may be helpful.

One of the principal differences in the Owen/Rosenberg contrast is that Owen's poems are, in the main, recollected. 'It seemed that out of battle I escaped.' 'But cursed are dullards whom no cannon stuns' (an allusion to the insensitive civilian); this latter, it is true, is recollected in anger rather than tranquillity, but even so, recollected. Something of Owen's Wordsworthian character is re-inforced in this distancing (which Wordsworth did not always employ); whereas with 'Dead Man's Dump', and, in a different but also powerful way, with 'Daughters of War', Rosenberg's experience is, in a sense, actually being enacted. 'Here is one not long dead'; 'Space beats the ruddy freedom of their limbs . . . My sisters have their males.' In this mode Rosenberg shares, for instance, the actuality of Coleridge's *Ancient Mariner* in that the story told happens now, in all its vividness. It is also Blake's mode in the *Songs of Innocence and Experience* – and

Lawrence's – and in adverting to Blake, we touch on one of Rosenberg's influences (we recall that, like Blake, Rosenberg was also a painter, if far inferior to Blake in this talent). That influence gets shown us in 'Break of Day in the Trenches' where Blake's 'The Echoing [darkening] Green' (*Songs of Innocence*) is both paralleled and ironically juxtaposed with 'the sleeping green between', which is both the soldiers' sleep and their no-man's land between the trenches; it is also, of course, their sleep *between* combat.

One curious aspect of this Owen/Rosenberg antinomy is that Owen recollects, with 'Strange Meeting', in narrative form, while Rosenberg moves steadily over the battle field of 'Dead Man's Dump' with no apparent direction, until the same despairing conclusion is reached as Owen achieves in 'Strange Meeting'. Rosenberg's (Coleridgean) energy moves through a series of crises, each of which occasions a density of language, even a new richness, altogether different from Owen's more evenly continuous narration. Compare

Then, as I probed them, one sprang up, and stared
With piteous recognition in fixed eyes,
Lifting distressful hands, as if to bless.
And by his smile, I knew that sullen hall,
By his dead smile I knew we stood in Hell.

with

What fierce imaginings their dark souls lit?
Earth! have they gone into you!
Somewhere they must have gone,
And flung on your hard back
Is their soul's sack
Emptied of God-ancestralled essences.
Who hurled them out? Who hurled?

Even though Owen's lines are concerned with one person, while Rosenberg is, for once, attempting a synoptic view of the dead in war, Rosenberg's lines do have a fierce immediacy not present in Owen's. Perhaps this is in part to do with the fineness of sensuous meaning. At first sight, for instance, it will seem as though the 'soul's sack' is the body; but I think the image suggests the finer idea, namely, that the soul itself has a sack, as the unborn child is not merely contained within the body, but inside its own amnion. This finer apprehension makes all the more tragic and wanton the disposal of the precious soul, which is meanwhile unceremoniously dumped on to earth's 'hard back'. This renders the slaughter even more dire, it is the destruction of a civilization's spiritual life; and it reaches absolute calamity in the line

Emptied of God-ancestralled essences.

These are the essential constituents, or nuclei, of the soul, and it's these that get evacuated. Hurled out. The language here is dense: both 'God' and 'ancestralled' are adjectival, although one is a noun, the other the passive form of the past participle. But the power of God drives the passive form which itself derives impetus from its "to ancestor", its long process of generation having God as its initiator. The passivity of our primal initiation is contrasted with the passive experience of being murdered; for it is these God-created, God-tinctured essences, precisely, that are hurled out. The kinds of unanswerable questions implied correspond to those asked in the last three lines of Owen's 'Futility':

Was it for this the clay grew tall?
– O what made fatuous sunbeams toil
To break earth's sleep at all?

Owen's lines are not better than Rosenberg's for being more explicit. As with Owen, the question in Rosenbergian terms is put in religious form; the connections between,

and even the partial inhering of, the generative powers of
God and Humanity are made explicit, and made powerful.
These too are destroyed, but the point of Rosenberg's
language is that vitality of a powerful and sacred order is
released as war expels the vitalities from the soul's sack
(and the soul). At any rate, they are also expelled from the
body through which alone we may experience these
essences. In Judaic terms, in fact, although the soul may
be nucleated by God's essences, humanity can only
experience these through the body, that is, the total
being; for in earthly life body and essences are inseparable.

Rosenberg's language then – this may seem strangely
put – is more lived in than Owen's. Owen's language
narrates or carries the ideas; Rosenberg's language is
them, sensuously enacts them, and experiences them. So
to this extent it shares some of the 'haecceity' (or thisness)
of Jones's language.

But there's a crucial difference. I do not know whether
the difference proceeds from Jones's religious character,
or from Catholicism, to which he became a convert in
1921; whichever way it is, Jones believed that the sacra-
mental (sign-making) act, that of making, or re-presenting,
was parallel to the rites of Catholicism. As he puts it in
'Art and Sacrament'[1]

Because the Church is committed to 'Sacraments' with a
capital S, she cannot escape a committal to sacrament with a
small s.

So the signs and rites of the Church are not only represent-
ative of but also become, at a certain stage, the flesh and
blood of Christ, that is, the things represented. And
although, logically, it does not follow that art therefore
assumes the "flesh" of the things it represents, there is for

[1] *Epoch and Artist.*

Jones such magic in the language that this is what may (for him) be assumed to be happening. The effect of this, however, is paradoxical for instead of promoting a metaphysical depth and extra spiritual dimension to his work, which Rosenberg's undoubtedly has, Jones's work tends to remain within its own haecceity, precisely because he believes that the bread and wine turn into the flesh and blood instead of remaining on the level of symbolism. Transubstantiation defeats symbolism when it's believed in. And if I read Jones precisely, he does believe in it. At any rate, the effect on his work is as though he did. The precise density of language can be seen in

He watches where you lift a knee joint gingerly, to avoid
low obstacles,
with flexed articulation poked
from young leaves parted
  – and plug and splinter
shin and fibula
and twice-dye with crimson moistening
for draggled bloodwort and the madder sorrel.
                                      – *In Parenthesis*, 7

When it comes to the Queen of the Woods whose beautiful elegy for the dead soldiers it is that concludes *In Parenthesis*, we do not have, in the language, symbolic resonance so much as a literal-minded (and occasionally punning) allegory: -

  Ulrich smiles for his myrtle wand.
  That swine Lillywhite has daisies to his chain – you'd hardly credit it.
  She plaits torques of equal splendour for Mr Jenkins and Billy Crower.
                                      – *In Parenthesis*, 7

The words have taken on not so much symbolic depth as the craftsmanly otherness of the things they would

ordinarily signify. Something is strangely awry here, and I
believe it's because the words have been required to do
what is beyond the capacity of language; that is, they
cannot transform themselves into the things they signify;
that would be magic, not religion. It can't of course be
other than speculation, but this fluidity, in which the
things signified and their language move in and out of
each other, appears, in its turn, to correspond to Jones's
fluidity of form in which there is little formal distinction, in
In Parenthesis, between prose and verse. The distinction
is there, but it's in the intensity, which is of primary
importance in the work.

With that said it may seem curious that, after David
Jones, the poet the critic John H. Johnston most reveres is
Herbert Read; but this is because Read uses a form which
is in some way remotely contingent on epic which, in its
turn, is itself remotely concomitant with the categorical
imperatives of duty. This he is especially strong on. In
rebuking Sassoon, Johnston says that: 'he could hardly
portray a soldier mastering his own turmoil and respond-
ing to the imperatives of duty. To write such things would
have been to grant that the war had some positive moral or
historical significance.'[1] In as much as Jones's testimony
of war is ambiguous (consider the boast 'I was there' in
In Parenthesis, pp. 79–84); and Read's long poem *The End
of a War*, which Yeats included in his *Oxford Book of
Modern Verse*, sets out some of the ways in which duty
operates, whatever its conclusions, these poems get
Johnston's approval. This is odd, for Jones and Read share
very little else, especially as we consider the kinds of
language they use. I believe Read's poem is, after Rosen-
berg's work, the most under-rated poem to be written out
of an experience of the war; and his language is at the
other end of the spectrum from Jones's. Read's language is

[1] John H. Johnston, *English Poetry of the First World War*, p. 102.

the language of ideas despite his attachment to imagism.[1]
Yet notwithstanding the abstractness of Read's language,
the ideas in *The End of a War* (1933) are espoused with
such intensity that what gradually emerges is the most
delicate sensuousness of all which is of, or contingent on,
the ideas themselves:

> When the last jump comes
> and the axe-head blackness slips through flesh
> that welcomes it with open but unquivering lips
> then I shall be one with the Unknown . . .

The movement of line three, with its rhythmic disturbance,
enacts the beheading (as well as a stoic firmness in the face
of death); but the source of sensuous strength lies not in
this, as it turns out, but in its being a metaphor for an idea.
The metaphor itself breathes with the life of the idea it's
enacting. This is extremely delicate writing, but the delic-
acy can't be located by thinking of the image of the axe
and decapitation, and then perceiving the fineness with
which this is (or is not) expressed. The sensuousness
emerges only, and as soon, as one perceives the idea which
the metaphor is subservient to and that the shock thus re-
created isn't a part of a physical apprehension, but the
mind's shock, as it thinks. The delicacy is located in the
movement of the thinking mind. I can't tell how much of
this Read was conscious of, but there's no indication by
Yeats that he was aware of it either. The sensuousness, at
any rate, results from Read being under the pressure of
unusually terrible experience and being put by it to
respond in his most characteristic mode, which is thought,
rather than sensuous enactment.

Read's minor mode is imagism – 'The Happy Warrior'[2],
for instance – and with this mode, a more prose-like
version of it, one associates the more successful poems of

---

[1] See Read's *Collected Poems*, p. 274.
[2] Consider its adverse judgement on Wordsworth's 'Character of the
Happy Warrior'.

Aldington and the few that Ford did not write apropos of the war effort.

Finally we are left with nature and war, and the language poets found with which to fit the two together.[1] Hardy has an almost unbearably sensitive apprehension of war's destruction of nature, in *The Dynasts*, which I should quote in full. It is on the eve of Waterloo:

Chorus of the Years

Yea, the coneys are scared by the thud of hoofs,
And their white scuts flash at their vanishing heels,
And swallows abandon the hamlet-roofs.

The mole's tunnelled chambers are crushed by wheels,
The lark's eggs scattered, their owners fled;
And the hedgehog's household the sapper unseals.

The snail draws in at the terrible tread,
But in vain; he is crushed by the felloe-rim;
The worm asks what can be overhead,

And wriggles deep from a scene so grim,
And guesses him safe; for he does not know
What a foul red flood will be soaking him!

Beaten about by the heel and toe
Are butterflies, sick of the day's long rheum,
To die of a worse than the weather-foe.

Trodden and bruised to a miry tomb
Are ears that have greened but will never be gold,
And flowers in the bud that will never bloom.

— Part Third, VI, viii

In many ways the best prose to come out of the struggle is Blunden's *Undertones of War* (1928), and throughout the work Blunden juxtaposes war and nature in such a manner that they seem, on some occasions at least, interchangeable – to the *senses*. The noise of gnats, and bullets,

---

[1] For an account of how Owen uses nature as moral preceptress and judge see this writer's *Out of Battle*, pp. 202–6 and 215–16.

resemble each other. Blunden is thus able to interpenetrate
the experience of the one with the other; the bullets are
'whizzing like gnats' he tells us. The word 'like' points the
difference, however, and indicates that experience informs
the intelligence of the contrary condition whereby gnats
and bullets exist. That a one-way penetration is complete,
to the disservice of nature, can be gathered from 'Report
on Experience':

I have seen a green country, useful to the race,
Knocked silly with guns and mines, its villages vanished . . .

And how devastating this is, as a "fact", and as an experi-
ence of the fact, may be seen from the analogy that informs
the whole poem, in which not only womanhood is cor-
rupted, but innocence disillusioned for ever.

Again, a fine account of Blunden's poetry is given by
Leavis[1]:

There was also in his poems, for all their rich rusticity, the
home-spun texture that is their warrant, a frank literary
quality . . . out of the traditional life of the English countryside,
especially as relived in memories of childhood, Mr Blunden was
creating a world – a world in which to find refuge from adult
distresses; above all, one guessed, from memories of the war . . .
There [is] something satisfying about the dense richness of his
pastoral world . . . He was able to be, to some purpose, con-
servative in technique, and to draw upon the eighteenth
century, because the immemorial rural order that is doomed
was real to him.

From this one may gratefully expand the hint approxi-
mated in what is located as eighteenth-century nature
pastoralized.

By these means Blunden is able to bring together war
and nature, not infrequently under the sometimes gentle if
stringent yoke of – of all things – humour. Wry it often is,
but it is humour. The undermost layers of this humour are

[1] *New Bearings in English Poetry*, pp. 59–61.

harsh, as how can they not be. Only the foolishly innocent and ignorant are deceived. Finally war destroys all that is valuable to humanity, for nature is man's moral preceptress. The only exchange for that is useless understanding. There is no joke. This complicated batting to and fro of sensuous innuendo and moral despair forms the core of Blunden's best war poems. It's there, and it's potent.

OWEN'S METRICS AND HIS COMPASSION

4

To return from Blunden to Owen is to re-enter an area of debate.

I was a German conscript, and your friend

and

I am the enemy you killed, my friend

are, as has been remarked, two versions of the famous line from Owen's 'Strange Meeting'. They reflect the limits of Owen's poetic oscillation between the mode of physical particularity (Sassoon's) and the universal one. As I've suggested, a small but recognizable part of Owen's adult practice as a poet tends to tie in with the rather grandiose and portentous response *officially* given in England to compassion. Compare this with the crucial moment in the Scottish poet Henryson's *Testament of Cresseid*.[1] The (southern) English tendency is to elevate compassion into a religiose sentiment, and thus remove it from the earth, making innocuous any inquiry as to the state of the victim and the cause of his suffering that a more earth-bound and singular tenderness might have made.[2] It is at once politically expedient and morally less taxing as a mode. This version of saccharine pity comes over, for instance,

---

[1] Lines 498–504.
[2] And yet at least compassion is recognized as a desirable attribute of the official pantheon.

very strongly in Britten's *War Requiem*. It is safely collated with bits of the Mass (which does no good to the Mass either), the total effect of which is to reinforce the weaker elements in Owen's poetry which might be conveniently summarized as the 'sad shires' syndrome ('Anthem for Doomed Youth'). Like 'the kind old sun' in 'Futility' – is it irony or sentimentality – this line, as one of my students suggested, might be read with the kind of irony that remarks: indeed the shires are sad at being depopulated, don't you know:

And bugles calling for them from sad shires.

But the first line in the succeeding sestet does not promote that reading in my mind; it's tonally full of "Oh the sadness of it all":

What candles may be held to speed them all?

Owen's achievement is sensitive at precisely this point – of 'sad shires'. Apparently I am not the only one to think so, for despite his admonition that we should not seek to characterize Owen as a 'war poet' – or as any *kind* of poet – but only as poet (page 5), by page 27 Dominic Hibberd offers this in his British Council monograph[1]: 'It is important, in any consideration of Owen's achievement, to remember that he was above all an elegist; that is to say, his major poems are laments for the dead rather than exposures of the horrors of war.' Hibberd is over-scrupulous about protecting his flank, as the qualification 'major poems' suggests. There may be poems other than elegies in Owen's (war) *oeuvre*, he tells us, but these are not his major achievements. Such camouflage is tedious, and by offering the contrasting characterization of 'elegist' Hibberd in any case restricts Owen's poetic character more severely than the term 'war poet' does. It attempts to ignore the Sassoon-like mode in Owen, and in so doing places undue stress on, indeed approves, the 'sad shires' syndrome. Thus in

[1] *Wilfred Owen*, 1974.

denying to Owen the Sassoon-like mode, in wishing to deny, that is, any desire on Owen's part to expose the horrors of war, Hibberd seriously weakens Owen's achievement, at precisely that point where Owen was strengthening himself. No harm comes from reminding ourselves that so keen was Owen to disclose the horrors of war to the civilian mind that he would carry with him photographs of wounded soldiers, and, at the appropriate moment of civilian obtuseness, would produce this evidence.[1] Such is not the character of an elegist, and it would be right to suggest that this activity of disclosure, which is surely something that was strengthened, at least, by Sassoon's example, finds its poetic counterpart in a number of Owen's poems. That Owen was aware of the Sassoon-like mode in his work may, at the very least, be indicated by citing his letter to Leslie Gunston (22 August 1917) where he says of his (earlier draft of) 'The Dead-Beat', 'after leaving him, I wrote something in Sassoon's style'. That is indeed so, and this (candid) rightly unabashed admission of his absorption of another's poetic attributes puts us directly on to the poems in 'Sassoon's style', major or no. 'Dulce Et Decorum Est' and in an altogether different mode 'The Show' are obvious instances; but 'The Sentry' is hardly less so, and nor is 'The Chances'. To which one might add 'The Last Laugh', 'The Letter', 'S.I.W.'; and of the results of war 'À Terre' and 'Mental Cases'. 'Disabled' also owes something to Sassoon. And for satire the first seventeen lines of 'Smile, Smile, Smile', amongst the last of Owen's poems, are written in precisely that incisive mode which is

[1] See *Appendix* by Frank Nicholson in Blunden's edition of *The Poems*, pp. 134–5.

  In fact, in a lecture given on 26 November 1977 (at Bolton), Dominic Hibberd declared that in his opinion there was no evidence to support the supposed existence of such photographs and that he did not believe they had ever existed. That may be; but there is enough Sassoon-like pugnacity in a number of Owen's poems to flesh the myth, true or false.

so telling in Sassoon. Whether or not any of these are 'major poems', I would add that this list can be extended; moreover there are enough poems in Sassoon's style to disturb the characterization of 'elegist' which Hibberd would impose on Owen.[1] It is perhaps needless to suggest that this Sassoon-like impulse is not confined to these poems, and in varying degrees it balances the compassion in poems such as 'Insensibility' ('But cursed are dullards'). It is with Sassoon's mode that we may see Owen's desire to reduce or change those circumstances which produce war and thus the conditions of suffering and murder. The elegist sentimentalizes the picture if he only mourns; he must additionally indicate that those who suffer also cause an identical suffering in others. To do this, however, is to exchange the role of 'elegist' for something more searching and effectual. This Owen did in 'Strange Meeting'. It would have been surprising if a poet of Owen's calibre had not succeeded in freeing himself from this kind of elegizing which, as I believe, constitutes a weakness in Owen when it is allowed to operate in an exclusive way. So far from wishing to accept this as a full characterization of Owen, I should want to suggest therefore that *where* it occurs there the reader must most of all be on his or her guard.

Owen is of course a more complex poet than the term 'elegist' allows; and in his attempt to shear Owen (and

---

[1] It may be we should trust the tale not the teller; but shouldn't we trust the teller more than the critic? In Owen's analytic "table of contents", he cites the poems and their 'Motive'. Against the heading of 'Motive' ten poems receive the designation 'Protest'. Another, 'Heroic lies'; another, 'Inhumanity of war'; another, 'Indifference at home'; another, 'The insupportability of war'; and another, 'Foolishness of war' ('Strange Meeting'); and yet another, 'Horrible beastliness of war'. In a different category – 'Philosophy' – a number of terms occur; the last of which, seemingly added as an afterthought, is 'Disgust'. None of these, at least, sounds like the expressions of an 'elegist'.

poor Shelley) of politics, Hibberd stresses another critical
mode, and aspires to another account of Owen, which has
its pitfalls. Such a mode is perceptible even in the caution
of such work as Welland's; and it shows its hand when
Welland "psychologizes" the 'enemy' in Owen's 'Strange
Meeting' as Owen's 'alter ego'.[1] Hibberd's approach,
which owes something to Welland at this point, could also
be characterized as psychological (and sometimes incon-
sistent).[2] In such a "psychiatrized" account we find (in
both pieces) frequent references to Owen's mother and
her strong effect on her son. This is not in itself exception-
able, but it does distort Hibberd's account of 'Spring
Offensive' which is, according to Hibberd, Owen's last
poem: 'The further image of the clinging brambles is
reminiscent of the embrace of the trees in 'Happiness';
Mrs Owen is present here, as so often . . . The breaking of
the maternal bond, the clinging brambles, is followed by
the making of war.'[3] If this seems obtrusive, the method
intensifies its reading in what follows:

> The final rejection of the clinging maternal arms and of
> passivity is heroic; there is an instant of exultation as the men
> challenge the sun and the landscape. There can be nothing
> Christian or Shelleyan about such an onslaught . . . but the
> offensive against the spring has not been wholly futile. Owen
> remained in the fighting line, confident and admired as an
> officer.

Much depends on how we read 'heroic'. One takes it that
the breaking of the maternal bonds is cited approvingly
as an image of Owen's maturation. It would follow that
the effort of this is 'heroic', and that the act of both
breaking the bonds and that of the attack are also to be
read as 'heroic'. But here the non-value-making psycho-

[1] *Wilfred Owen: A Critical Study*, p. 100 ff.
[2] See for instance 'Images of Darkness in the Poems of Wilfred
Owen', *Durham University Journal*, March 1974.
[3] ibid., pp. 38–9.

logical exegesis finds itself in difficulties; for although it
may be possible to cite the discarding of the maternal
bonds approvingly (if that is what the pushing aside of
the brambles constitutes) it is not possible to attribute
such a positive to its counterpart which is the attack itself;
the *poem* will not permit such a reading –

>   And instantly the whole sky burned
> With fury against them.

It may therefore be that the original "psychologizing"
exegesis is at fault. Indeed it may, because if we are to
read the activity with this non-value-making approval, we
must deny Owen everything he had up till then concluded
about war. To characterize Owen in his maturity as a
'confident . . . officer' does not altogether do justice to
Owen even if he was concerned to discharge the stigma of
'cowardice' and fight honourably, as befits an officer. It
does not take account of Owen's conflict as he expressed it
in the line already given from a letter to his mother of
May 1917: 'And am I not myself a conscientious objector
with a very seared conscience?' In 1918, Hibberd tells us,
'Germany showed that she had lost none of her ambitions.
Having finally subdued her Eastern Front, she launched a
massive offensive westwards.'[1] Did Owen's maturity con-
sist in opposing this (supposedly one-sided) ambitious-
ness?

A different variety of such not altogether helpful
Englishness may be seen in the inclusion by Larkin (or
Thwaite) of 'Anthem for Doomed Youth' in *The Oxford
Book of Twentieth Century English Verse*. This poem fits
such a canonization, but in being so conscripted harms
Owen's compassion such as is found in all its strength in
'Insensibility'. This latter, it's fair to say, is the first item
in this anthology's representation of Owen, and so one

[1] ibid., p. 31.

questions the sensibility which includes both poems. This 'sad shires' version of compassion also, as I've suggested, brings into some question the authenticity of the religious despair, courage and acceptance within the Mass when it is placed alongside it (as it is in Britten's *Requiem*); it disembodies those attributes which the Mass embodies.

Thus the first version of the line from 'Strange Meeting' (above) reinforces the mode of particularized compassion (the more I live with this line the more I see going for it). Whereas the second line could be used – ripped from its context – stuffed into some 'larger' preamble – to reinforce the portentous celebration of our dead (who is 'our' in this context?). Much could be said about these manoeuvres, oddly enough, by showing what features they share with the Larkin (and Thwaite) anthology. Thus, to digress more, the selection[1] – and I don't only mean the kind of *inclusions* of post-second-war poems – tends to open itself to the sort of criticism one might make of Larkin's English lyricism; at any rate, the kind of lyricism which, if put to it, he's not averse to; and which might fairly be represented by Auden's 'Yeats' and his unnecessarily cruel 'Miss Gee'; by the impassioned beauty of Yeats himself; by some of Hardy; by De La Mare; by a sizeable chunk of Graves, and of course Betjeman. Not but that we aren't talking about some "good poetry"; but it's all a question (or largely) of emphasis. It can be adverted to by referring to the peripheral choices made of Rosenberg ('August 1914'

---

[1] Larkin writes in his Preface, pp. v–vi:

> In making my selection I have striven to hold a balance between all the different considerations that press on anyone understanding a book of this kind . . . [and of the poets born after 1914] wide rather than deep representation, and . . . I have acted not so much critically, or even historically, but as someone wanting to bring together poems that will give pleasure to their readers both separately and as a collection.

and 'Louse Hunting'; the would-have-been "damaging" inclusions of 'Dead Man's Dump' and 'Break of Day in the Trenches' are, significantly enough, not made). To balance the kind of lyrical nexus, which I'm attempting to profile, there are included the satires of intellect as represented, for instance, by Sassoon; which inclusions seem to attempt a critical balance by an evening of the odds, a balance which would not have been achieved by a more thorough-going "lyrical" selection. But the significant way in which the would-be balance is sought for (through the "intellect" of the as-it-were "opposition") and not through the real and corresponding strengths of the opposition, is telling. Had the job been done properly, for instance, it would have included the two Rosenberg poems noted as absent (above) for this would have got into the anthology a sensuous commitment, the presence of which is far more representative of the strengths of the opposition than Sassoon. Such a true opposition would have included Herbert Read's 'The End of a War' (or some of it), something from Bunting's *Briggflatts* rather than his earlier and more "intellectual" 'Chomei at Toyama'; and it would have excluded Geoffrey Hill's unrepresentative 'In Memory of Jane Fraser' for the (one-would-have-thought) unmissable 'September Song'. This last takes up a 'foreign' subject, and is therefore perhaps not a thoroughly English poem; but setting aside that little contretemps, what I'm pointing to is the omission of those poems whose animus, bias, or positive is not English (or Anglo-Irish) lyric, and whose *virtu* lies in their sensuous intelligence which reaches beyond, or under, song. But the omissions go beyond any single version of damage; omission is one thing, but imbalance causes a different distress because it creates a context in which – and I testify to this from my reading – even the positively intelligent sensuousness of poems such as Lawrence's 'Song of a Man Who Has Come Through' appear as the slightly eccentric museum-pieces of passion that they, or at any rate this, really aren't. That this kind of distortion happens I can attest to, where the same poem, in a different context, appears rather, if not altogether, different and, in the preferred context, not disappointing. Of course, it could be argued that the context I am objecting to is the "right one", and that it serves to bring out the essential weakness of such passionate utterance. One reply to this might be that the context in which this supposed "bringing out of weakness" occurs is itself unbalanced. This is not merely a case of collars versus rolled shirt sleeves, and how much passion may be found below the collar isn't for me to say. The issue can be more positively apprehended by saying that when it comes to Blake's *Songs of Innocence and Experience*, Burns's 'Holy Willie's Prayer', or Wordsworth's 'The Solitary Reaper' or 'Resolution and Independence' – that despite the political message of "patience dear man" in that last, we don't, in these poems, consider the problem in terms of shirt sleeves or collars.

This may seem a long way round to get at the two versions of Owen's line from 'Strange Meeting', but if, as I believe we are, we're considering the accumulated social pressures that Owen's versions verbalize, then this kind of analysis isn't as discursive as it may at first seem. At any rate some preliminary clearing of the ground seemed to me necessary so that the reader might consider what's involved. For myself, what's involved, which I want to touch on, is the sensuous nature of the versions, which can be approached through their rhythms.

There's a line in Keats's 'To Autumn' in which the disposition of one syllable gives a crucial reading, and thus in this dense-packed poem, to the whole work:

While barrèd clouds bloom the soft-dying day.

With the usual reading of 'barred', one would have to prolong the vowels of 'soft-dying' in order to obtain an

iambic pentameter, which is what all the other lines in the
poem patently demand of this. But such a reading exag-
gerates the "typically" Keatsean sensuousness and gives
the game to the bloodless pastoralist. Death is in that kind
of reading the easiest exchange of all for life. That is not
however where I think the metrical stress falls. With a
little archaic licence, which you might have obtained
more easily then than now, we can read 'barred' as
'barrèd'. As soon as the word gets a double syllable, the
metrical stress falls, more or less as it ought, on 'bloom';
with the proviso that one of course reverses the iamb
/bloom the/so that 'the' doesn't receive a simple mechanical
(and unsayable) stress. And as a matter of fact, by re-
positioning the stress on to 'bloom' one gets it right; for
one draws attention, with the help of the metrical irregu-
larity, to the implications of the important word 'bloom':
summer's fruit gives itself to autumn, clouds bloom their
(sunset) colour from the dying sun. Which reminds one
that middle-age's maturity lies between the fulness of
summer and winter death. The three cycles of nature, day,
and man are thus meshed through one's being able to
stress 'bloom'.

I haven't unravelled all the implications of the word, and
here isn't the place for it. All I now want to draw attention
to is how crucial can be the positioning of a stress, or the
placing of a pause, in a metrical system. Not that the
reader should gather from the tone here that this is thought
to be earth-shaking revelation. But it serves to re-introduce
the disjunctions I was identifying in the versions of
Owen's compassion, and the social impulses they tended
to dramatize; it required all of Owen's strength and tact
to prevent the two impulses – of the 'sad shires' and
paternalism – reverting to their basic polarities.

I was/a Ger/man con/script, and/your friend

There (mechanically, one might object) is the line put into

five feet. And here's the later version which erases the above:

I am/the en/emy/you killed/,my friend

One notices about the two versions that the first takes longer to *say*; the second is, one might argue, for that reason, more conversational, and thus, better. To quote Wilde on the inauguration of a telephone system between London and New York, and of how good that was, 'It depends on the quality of the conversation.'

One notices in the first version how the stresses fall on 'I', 'Ger(man)' and on 'con(script)' and 'friend'. The metrical stresses set up the paradoxical nature of the (all) conflict. He was *made* to fight and kill (he didn't really want to); thus 'conscript' is fully metrically weighted against 'friend' with the intended ironic paradox. Moreover, the comma in this line, coming between 'conscript' and 'and', enacts the ironic emphasis obtained the moment the disparate elements are joined; and it's important that the dramatic hesitation occurs in the middle of a foot, thus further slowing the whole line into sensuous enactment.

The second, final version, for all its impressiveness, doesn't do *that* kind of enactment. You may say that the universality of this version more than compensates for the loss. I'm not sure. In this second version the primary stresses are on 'killed' and 'friend' (Shelley's 'We are all brethren') thereby getting the line system to enact a less complex irony, a more literary paradox, than the first version. The second is more obviously dramatic; but is that to its benefit? Moreover the comma, in this version, occurs *between* the penultimate and last foot; by pausing between them, more "aloneness" is given to the little phrase 'my friend' which, in its paradoxicality, imparts a tone of solemnity (and, dare one say it, a touch of the portentous, if read in a certain way) rather than the irony *and* pain of 'and your friend' of the first version. These are the problems raised by the two lines, or some of them.

THE POEMS

5

To account for one's choice will perhaps seem like self-pleading, but such accounting may also be taken as an outlining of the principles by which the poets were chosen. To start with, then, the barest historical requirement was that the poetry should have been to do with the war, and have been written by those who lived in, or through, the period. Nothing more seemed needed. Rosenberg, Owen, Sassoon, and Blunden were, for instance, combatants; Flint and Pound were not. Rosenberg, Owen, and Sorley were killed; Read and Blunden survived. Thomas wrote poetry impinged on by the war, but wrote nothing after arriving for a brief service on the Western Front. Almost all Owen's "war" poetry was written after his initiation to combat on the Western Front. Rosenberg wrote his play *Moses* between enlistment and service in France – 'written since I joined' – as he puts it to Marsh. But although the bulk of the "war" poetry post-dates his arrival in France, significant apprehensions regarding war pre-date that. David Jones's *In Parenthesis* and Herbert Read's 'The End of a War' were written after the war, perhaps, in both their cases, without any prior expectation of the works being produced. Ungaretti wrote and fought on the Isonzo Front (between Italy and Austria); and came through. Which brings in the delicate question of translation.

Of course I must seem to be contradicting myself when I say on the one hand that I am not concerned with historical principles, and on the other, claim that only by having (a little) work in translation can one more fully recognize the variety of response in the English poetry of the period. But of course I do mean what I say. The anthology is not organized on historical principles. There is not a-poem-a-person from everyone-who-wrote during the war. Nor are the different phases of the war – even though these may be said to exist – dutifully represented by the appropriate poems. Much as the word may rightly be challenged, I was in the end concerned with excellence, not the representation of extrinsic concerns. These concerns of course impinge *within* the poems, but they neither necessarily make nor mar them. A concern with the substance of war, with the terrifying combat, pervades my choices; but most good poetry keeps close to the experiential rather than to abstraction. So in the end I had to choose what I thought was good; and if I thought the poem good it was included. Desmond Graham introduced me to Frederic Manning's *Eidolon* (the writer of *Her Privates We*) and there's a poem by him here. There are two poems by Brooke, but none by Herbert Asquith. There is work by Kipling, and by Rosenberg. There aren't a large number of different poets in the anthology, but there are greatly different poetries.

Apart from Brooke, who appears as the representative of Georgian poetics – if that isn't unjust – and of that patriotism which distinguished the opening phases of the war, the case rests, as it must, on excellence; and the reader will be correct in thinking that the more poems there are by a poet the more highly I think of him (translated works excepted).

There are thus a great many poems by Rosenberg, and by Owen. There are a considerable number by Thomas, Blunden and Sassoon. There is much from David Jones's *In Parenthesis*, and all of Herbert Read's 'The End of a War' is included (a much underrated poem, I think). Here is Hardy's very fine 'Channel Firing', but not his recruiting song 'Men who March Away'. And with regard to the

translated work, I obtained from poet-translators what
seemed poetry in English. In certain cases (like Trakl's)
I had a choice of versions; as I had with Ungaretti. In
other cases there was none. Even so, the reek of possible
error, on this score, will for some be present. But what of
it? Larkin has exclaimed 'Foreign Poetry' rather in the
way that Lady Bracknell queried the relevance of 'The
Brighton Line'. The lineage, I confess, is not important.
Of course one can be wrong; who can't be? But then one
can be wrong, with less excuse, about English poetry.
Surely the area isn't to be demarcated, so that as little error
as possible may be made; the area should be as fully as
possible explored for what, in the end, rejoices one. And
so it is; I rejoice in Rosenberg's 'Dead Man's Dump' even
more than I do in Owen's 'Insensibility' (the latter a poem
Dominic Hibberd can hardly accommodate). Thomas's
'As the Team's Head-Brass', 'Rain', and 'The Owl' are
so good that one forgets how fine Blunden is, and how
exacting his 'Report on Experience' remains. Who does
not smile with 'Base Details' and, *pace* Dennis Enright,
Sassoon's 'They'? The list is extendable, and the vigour
of the work won't be denied. What is also there, though
less often remarked on, is the delicacy. It's late to be
introducing a new approbating term, but it was Lawrence
who coupled vigour with delicacy as a mark of a good
poem. That's so, and delicacy with vigour, or on its own,
is found here. Tommy's tunes aren't all that contemptible.

As I've suggested, I did not want to offer an anthology
based on historical principles, but one where I made an
attempt at defining what I thought was excellent. Yet it's
clear that an anthology of First War poetry is, in a special
sense, also an anthology based on history because it offers
poetry in response to a cataclysmic set of similar events,
all of which have to do with combat, and which we still
respond to. Yet not only to do with combat, so, in this
sense, not only historical. But whatever delimiting one

sets out to do, it's clear that much of the work is, in certain ways, defined by a common response to a particular human catastrophe in a brief period of time. Brief, that is, in perspective. *Ought* one then to have concentrated on making a historical anthology? As to that, it has been done already, but no anthology as far as I know has tried to *limit* itself to excellence. Even so, there are certain poems that have embedded themselves in our consciousness – such as Brooke's 'If I should die' and Julian Grenfell's 'Into Battle'. Are they in our consciousness by virtue of their being excellent poems, or because they have caught, and held, the sense of an ethos? Brooke's 'The Soldier' is in the main body of the anthology – for a variety of reasons – but Grenfell's 'Into Battle' is here because the editor wished to offer a sample of "famous" poems without which no anthology of First War poetry would even try to claim that it fully responded to the war. Not that any anthology can fully respond; but it is in the nature of this anthology to try to offer – mostly what the editor prefers and a little of what he believes other people, a great many other people, have liked, even loved, as they responded to the horror and pity of war. That little is offered even where I dissented from the implied judgements of taste – but there it is. The following poems, denoted in the text by an asterisk after the title, fit the case I've just made. These are: Grenfell's 'Into Battle', John McCrae's 'In Flanders Fields', Alan Seeger's 'Rendezvous', Sorley's 'All the hills and vales along' and Owen's 'Anthem for Doomed Youth'.

Finally, I end, as I began, with a poem by an American – Stephen Crane:

Do Not Weep

Do not weep, maiden, for war is kind.
Because your lover threw wild hands towards the sky

And the affrighted steed ran on alone,
Do not weep.
War is kind.

  Hoarse, booming drums of the regiment,
  Little souls who thirst for fight,
  These men were born to drill and die,
  The unexplained glory flies above them,
  Great is the battle-god, great, and his kingdom –
  A field where a thousand corpses lie.

Do not weep, babe, for war is kind.
Because your father tumbled in the yellow trenches,
Raged at his breast, gulped and died,
Do not weep.
War is kind.

  Swift blazing flag of the regiment,
  Eagle with crest of red and gold,
  These men were born to drill and die.
  Point for them the virtue of slaughter,
  Make plain to them the excellence of killing
  And a field where a thousand corpses lie.

Mother whose heart hung humble as a button
On the bright splendid shroud of your son,
Do not weep.
War is kind.

                                        JON SILKIN

Channel Firing

That night your great guns, unawares,
Shook all our coffins as we lay,
And broke the chancel window-squares,
We thought it was the Judgment-day

And sat upright. While drearisome
Arose the howl of wakened hounds:
The mouse let fall the altar-crumb,
The worms drew back into the mounds,

The glebe cow drooled. Till God called, 'No;
It's gunnery practice out at sea
Just as before you went below;
The world is as it used to be:

'All nations striving strong to make
Red war yet redder. Mad as hatters
They do no more for Christés sake
Than you who are helpless in such matters.

'That this is not the judgment-hour
For some of them's a blessed thing,
For if it were they'd have to scour
Hell's floor for so much threatening . . .

'Ha, ha. It will be warmer when
I blow the trumpet (if indeed
I ever do; for you are men,
And rest eternal sorely need).'

So down we lay again. 'I wonder,
Will the world ever saner be,'
Said one, 'than when He sent us under
In our indifferent century!'

And many a skeleton shook his head.
'Instead of preaching forty year,'
My neighbour Parson Thirdly said,
'I wish I had stuck to pipes and beer.'

Again the guns disturbed the hour,
Roaring their readiness to avenge,
As far inland as Stourton Tower,
And Camelot, and starlit Stonehenge.
April 1914

Drummer Hodge[1]

I

They throw in Drummer Hodge, to rest
    Uncoffined – just as found:
His landmark is a kopje-crest
    That breaks the veldt around;
And foreign constellations west
    Each night above his mound.

II

Young Hodge the Drummer never knew –
    Fresh from his Wessex home –
The meaning of the broad Karoo,
    The Bush, the dusty loam,
And why uprose to nightly view
    Strange stars amid the gloam.

[1] This Boer War poem is included principally for the purpose of
  comparison with Rupert Brooke's 'The Soldier'.

III

Yet portion of that unknown plain
    Will Hodge for ever be;
His homely Northern breast and brain
    Grow to some Southern tree,
And strange-eyed constellations reign
    His stars eternally.

c. 1899

RUPERT BROOKE

From *1914*

IV The Dead

These hearts were woven of human joys and cares,
   Washed marvellously with sorrow, swift to mirth.
The years had given them kindness. Dawn was theirs,
   And sunset, and the colours of the earth.
These had seen movement, and heard music; known
   Slumber and waking; loved; gone proudly friended;
Felt the quick stir of wonder; sat alone;
   Touched flowers and furs and cheeks. All this is ended.

There are waters blown by changing winds to laughter
And lit by the rich skies, all day. And after,
   Frost, with a gesture, stays the waves that dance
And wandering loveliness. He leaves a white
   Unbroken glory, a gathered radiance,
A width, a shining peace, under the night.

V The Soldier

If I should die, think only this of me:
   That there's some corner of a foreign field
That is for ever England. There shall be
   In that rich earth a richer dust concealed;
A dust whom England bore, shaped, made aware,
   Gave, once, her flowers to love, her ways to roam,
A body of England's, breathing English air,
   Washed by the rivers, blest by suns of home.

And think, this heart, all evil shed away,
  A pulse in the eternal mind, no less
    Gives somewhere back the thoughts by England
      given;
Her sights and sounds; dreams happy as her day;
  And laughter, learnt of friends; and gentleness,
    In hearts at peace, under an English heaven.

November–December 1914

JULIAN GRENFELL

Into Battle*

The naked earth is warm with spring,
  And with green grass and bursting trees
Leans to the sun's gaze glorying,
  And quivers in the sunny breeze;
And life is colour and warmth and light,
  And a striving evermore for these;
And he is dead who will not fight;
  And who dies fighting has increase.

The fighting man shall from the sun
  Take warmth, and life from the glowing earth;
Speed with the light-foot winds to run,
  And with the trees to newer birth;
And find, when fighting shall be done,
  Great rest, and fullness after dearth.

All the bright company of Heaven
  Hold him in their high comradeship,
The Dog-Star, and the Sisters Seven,
  Orion's Belt and sworded hip.

The woodland trees that stand together,
  They stand to him each one a friend;
They gently speak in the windy weather;
  They guide to valley and ridge's end.

The kestrel hovering by day,
  And the little owls that call by night,
Bid him be swift and keen as they,
  As keen of ear, as swift of sight.

The blackbird sings to him, 'Brother, brother,
  If this be the last song you shall sing,
Sing well, for you may not sing another;
  Brother, sing.'

In dreary, doubtful, waiting hours,
  Before the brazen frenzy starts,
The horses show him nobler powers;
  O patient eyes, courageous hearts!

And when the burning moment breaks,
  And all things else are out of mind,
And only joy of battle takes
  Him by the throat, and makes him blind,

Through joy and blindness he shall know,
  Not caring much to know, that still
Nor lead nor steel shall reach him, so
  That it be not the Destined Will.

The thundering line of battle stands,
  And in the air death moans and sings;
But Day shall clasp him with strong hands,
  And Night shall fold him in soft wings.

In Flanders Fields*

In Flanders fields the poppies blow
Between the crosses, row on row,
    That mark our place; and in the sky
    The larks, still bravely singing, fly
Scarce heard amid the guns below.

We are the Dead. Short days ago
We lived, felt dawn, saw sunset glow,
    Loved and were loved, and now we lie
        In Flanders fields.

Take up our quarrel with the foe:
To you from failing hands we throw
    The torch; be yours to hold it high.
    If ye break faith with us who die
We shall not sleep, though poppies grow
        In Flanders fields.

Rendezvous*

I have a rendezvous with Death
At some disputed barricade,
When Spring comes back with rustling shade
And apple-blossoms fill the air –
I have a rendezvous with Death
When Spring brings back blue days and fair.

It may be he shall take my hand
And lead me into his dark land
And close my eyes and quench my breath –
It may be I shall pass him still.
I have a rendezvous with Death
On some scarred slope of battered hill,
When Spring comes round again this year
And the first meadow-flowers appear.

God knows 'twere better to be deep
Pillowed in silk and scented down,
Where love throbs out in blissful sleep,
Pulse nigh to pulse, and breath to breath,
Where hushed awakenings are dear . . .
But I've a rendezvous with Death
At midnight in some flaming town,
When Spring trips north again this year,
And I to my pledged word am true,
I shall not fail that rendezvous.

CHARLES HAMILTON SORLEY

'All the hills and vales along'*

All the hills and vales along
Earth is bursting into song,
And the singers are the chaps
Who are going to die perhaps.
    O sing, marching men,
      Till the valleys ring again.
      Give your gladness to earth's keeping,
      So be glad, when you are sleeping.

Cast away regret and rue,
Think what you are marching to.
Little live, great pass.
Jesus Christ and Barabbas
Were found the same day.
This died, that went his way.
    So sing with joyful breath,
      For why, you are going to death.
      Teeming earth will surely store
      All the gladness that you pour.

Earth that never doubts nor fears,
Earth that knows of death, not tears,
Earth that bore with joyful ease
Hemlock for Socrates,
Earth that blossomed and was glad
'Neath the cross that Christ had,
Shall rejoice and blossom too
When the bullet reaches you.
    Wherefore, men marching
      On the road to death, sing!

> Pour gladness on earth's head,
> So be merry, so be dead.

From the hills and valleys earth
Shouts back the sound of mirth,
Tramp of feet and lilt of song
Ringing all the road along.
All the music of their going,
Ringing swinging glad song-throwing,
Earth will echo still, when foot
Lies numb and voice mute.
> On marching men, on
> To the gates of death with song.
> Sow your gladness for earth's reaping,
> So you may be glad, though sleeping.
> Strew your gladness on earth's bed,
> So be merry, so be dead.

Two Sonnets

I

Saints have adored the lofty soul of you.
Poets have whitened at your high renown.
We stand among the many millions who
Do hourly wait to pass your pathway down.
You, so familiar, once were strange: we tried
To live as of your presence unaware.
But now in every road on every side
We see your straight and steadfast signpost there.

I think it like that signpost in my land,
Hoary and tall, which pointed me to go
Upward, into the hills, on the right hand,

Where the mists swim and the winds shriek and blow,
A homeless land and friendless, but a land
I did not know and that I wished to know.

II

Such, such is Death: no triumph: no defeat:
Only an empty pail, a slate rubbed clean,
A merciful putting away of what has been.

And this we know: Death is not Life effete,
Life crushed, the broken pail. We who have seen
So marvellous things know well the end not yet.

Victor and vanquished are a-one in death:
Coward and brave: friend, foe. Ghosts do not say
'Come, what was your record when you drew breath?'
But a big blot has hid each yesterday
So poor, so manifestly incomplete.
And your bright Promise, withered long and sped,
Is touched, stirs, rises, opens and grows sweet
And blossoms and is you, when you are dead.

12 June 1915

'When you see millions of the mouthless dead'

When you see millions of the mouthless dead
Across your dreams in pale battalions go,
Say not soft things as other men have said,
That you'll remember. For you need not so.
Give them not praise. For, deaf, how should they know
It is not curses heaped on each gashed head?
Nor tears. Their blind eyes see not your tears flow.
Nor honour. It is easy to be dead.
Say only this, 'They are dead.' Then add thereto,

'Yet many a better one has died before.'
Then, scanning all the o'ercrowded mass, should you
Perceive one face that you loved heretofore,
It is a spook. None wears the face you knew.
Great death has made all his for evermore.

A Private

This ploughman dead in battle slept out of doors
Many a frozen night, and merrily
Answered staid drinkers, good bedmen, and all bores:
'At Mrs Greenland's Hawthorn Bush', said he,
'I slept.' None knew which bush. Above the town,
Beyond 'The Drover', a hundred spot the down
In Wiltshire. And where now at last he sleeps
More sound in France – that, too, he secret keeps.

Man and Dog

''Twill take some getting.' 'Sir, I think 'twill so.'
The old man stared up at the mistletoe
That hung too high in the poplar's crest for plunder
Of any climber, though not for kissing under:
Then he went on against the north-east wind –
Straight but lame, leaning on a staff new-skinned,
Carrying a brolly, flag-basket, and old coat, –
Towards Alton, ten miles off. And he had not
Done less from Chilgrove where he pulled up docks.
'Twere best, if he had had 'a money-box',
To have waited there till the sheep cleared a field
For what a half-week's flint-picking would yield.
His mind was running on the work he had done
Since he left Christchurch in the New Forest, one
Spring in the 'seventies, – navvying on dock and line

From Southampton to Newcastle-on-Tyne, –
In 'seventy-four a year of soldiering
With the Berkshires, – hoeing and harvesting
In half the shires where corn and couch will grow.
His sons, three sons, were fighting, but the hoe
And reap-hook he liked, or anything to do with trees.
He fell once from a poplar tall as these:
The Flying Man they called him in hospital.
'If I flew now, to another world I'd fall.'
He laughed and whistled to the small brown bitch
With spots of blue that hunted in the ditch.
Her foxy Welsh grandfather must have paired
Beneath him. He kept sheep in Wales and scared
Strangers, I will warrant, with his pearl eye
And trick of shrinking off as he were shy,
Then following close in silence for – for what?
'No rabbit, never fear, she ever got,
Yet always hunts. To-day she nearly had one:
She would and she wouldn't. 'Twas like that. The
    bad one!
She's not much use, but still she's company,
Though I'm not. She goes everywhere with me.
So Alton I must reach to-night somehow:
I'll get no shakedown with that bedfellow
From farmers. Many a man sleeps worse to-night
Than I shall.' 'In the trenches.' 'Yes, that's right.
But they'll be out of that – I hope they be –
This weather, marching after the enemy.'
'And so I hope. Good luck.' And there I nodded
'Good-night. You keep straight on,' Stiffly he plodded;
And at his heels the crisp leaves scurried fast,
And the leaf-coloured robin watched. They passed,
The robin till next day, the man for good,
Together in the twilight of the wood.

The Owl

Downhill I came, hungry, and yet not starved;
Cold, yet had heat within me that was proof
Against the North wind; tired, yet so that rest
Had seemed the sweetest thing under a roof.

Then at the inn I had food, fire, and rest,
Knowing how hungry, cold, and tired was I.
All of the night was quite barred out except
An owl's cry, a most melancholy cry

Shaken out long and clear upon the hill,
No merry note, nor cause of merriment,
But one telling me plain what I escaped
And others could not, that night, as in I went.

And salted was my food, and my repose,
Salted and sobered, too, by the bird's voice
Speaking for all who lay under the stars,
Soldiers and poor, unable to rejoice.

In Memoriam (Easter, 1915)

The flowers left thick at nightfall in the wood
This Eastertide call into mind the men,
Now far from home, who, with their sweethearts, should
Have gathered them and will do never again.

Fifty Faggots

There they stand, on their ends, the fifty faggots
That once were underwood of hazel and ash
In Jenny Pinks's Copse. Now, by the hedge

Close packed, they make a thicket fancy alone
Can creep through with the mouse and wren. Next
    Spring
A blackbird or a robin will nest there,
Accustomed to them, thinking they will remain
Whatever is for ever to a bird:
This Spring it is too late; the swift has come.
'Twas a hot day for carrying them up:
Better they will never warm me, though they must
Light several Winters' fires. Before they are done
The war will have ended, many other things
Have ended, maybe, that I can no more
Foresee or more control than robin and wren.

This is No Case of Petty Right or Wrong

This is no case of petty right or wrong
That politicians or philosophers
Can judge. I hate not Germans, nor grow hot
With love of Englishmen, to please newspapers.
Beside my hate for one fat patriot
My hatred of the Kaiser is love true:–
A kind of god he is, banging a gong.
But I have not to choose between the two,
Or between justice and injustice. Dinned
With war and argument I read no more
Than in the storm smoking along the wind
Athwart the wood. Two witches' cauldrons roar.
From one the weather shall rise clear and gay;
Out of the other an England beautiful
And like her mother that died yesterday.
Little I know or care if, being dull,
I shall miss something that historians

Can rake out of the ashes when perchance
The phoenix broods serene above their ken.
But with the best and meanest Englishmen
I am one in crying, God save England, lest
We lose what never slaves and cattle blessed.
The ages made her that made us from dust:
She is all we know and live by, and we trust
She is good and must endure, loving her so:
And as we love ourselves we hate her foe.

Rain

Rain, midnight rain, nothing but the wild rain
On this bleak hut, and solitude, and me
Remembering again that I shall die
And neither hear the rain nor give it thanks
For washing me cleaner than I have been
Since I was born into this solitude.
Blessed are the dead that the rain rains upon:
But here I pray that none whom once I loved
Is dying to-night or lying still awake
Solitary, listening to the rain,
Either in pain or thus in sympathy
Helpless among the living and the dead,
Like a cold water among broken reeds,
Myriads of broken reeds all still and stiff,
Like me who have no love which this wild rain
Has not dissolved except the love of death,
If love it be for what is perfect and
Cannot, the tempest tells me, disappoint.

Roads

I love roads:
The goddesses that dwell
Far along invisible
are my favourite gods.

Roads go on
While we forget, and are
Forgotten like a star
That shoots and is gone.

On this earth 'tis sure
We men have not made
Anything that doth fade
So soon, so long endure:

The hill road wet with rain
In the sun would not gleam
Like a winding stream
If we trod it not again.

They are lonely
While we sleep, lonelier
For lack of the traveller
Who is now a dream only.

From dawn's twilight
And all the clouds like sheep
On the mountains of sleep
They wind into the night.

The next turn may reveal
Heaven: upon the crest
The close pine clump, at rest
And black, may Hell conceal.

Often footsore, never
Yet of the road I weary,

Though long and steep and dreary,
As it winds on for ever.

Helen of the roads,
The mountain ways of Wales
And the Mabinogion tales
Is one of the true gods,

Abiding in the trees,
The threes and fours so wise,
The larger companies,
That by the roadside be,

And beneath the rafter
Else uninhabited
Excepting by the dead;
And it is her laughter

At morn and night I hear
When the thrush cock sings
Bright irrelevant things,
And when the chanticleer

Calls back to their own night
Troops that make loneliness
With their light footsteps' press,
As Helen's own are light.

Now all roads lead to France
And heavy is the tread
Of the living; but the dead
Returning lightly dance:

Whatever the road bring
To me or take from me,
They keep me company
With their pattering,

Crowding the solitude
Of the loops over the downs,
Hushing the roar of towns
And their brief multitude.

February Afternoon

Men heard this roar of parleying starlings, saw,
    A thousand years ago even as now,
    Black rooks with white gulls following the plough
So that the first are last until a caw
Commands that last are first again, – a law
    Which was of old when one, like me, dreamed how
    A thousand years might dust lie on his brow
Yet thus would birds do between hedge and shaw.

Time swims before me, making as a day
    A thousand years, while the broad ploughland oak
    Roars mill-like and men strike and bear the stroke
    Of war as ever, audacious or resigned,
And God still sits aloft in the array
    That we have wrought him, stone-deaf and stone-
        blind.

The Cherry Trees

The cherry trees bend over and are shedding,
On the old road where all that passed are dead,
Their petals, strewing the grass as for a wedding
This early May morn when there is none to wed.

As the Team's Head-Brass

As the team's head-brass flashed out on the turn
The lovers disappeared into the wood.
I sat among the boughs of the fallen elm
That strewed the angle of the fallow, and
Watched the plough narrowing a yellow square
Of charlock. Every time the horses turned
Instead of treading me down, the ploughman leaned
Upon the handles to say or ask a word,
About the weather, next about the war.
Scraping the share he faced towards the wood,
And screwed along the furrow till the brass flashed
Once more.
      The blizzard felled the elm whose crest
I sat in, by a woodpecker's round hole,
The ploughman said, 'When will they take it away?'
'When the war's over.' So the talk began –
One minute and an interval of ten,
A minute more and the same interval.
'Have you been out?' 'No.' 'And don't want to, perhaps?'
'If I could only come back again, I should.
I could spare an arm. I shouldn't want to lose
A leg. If I should lose my head, why, so,
I should want nothing more . . . Have many gone
From here?' 'Yes.' 'Many lost?' 'Yes, a good few.
Only two teams work on the farm this year.
One of my mates is dead. The second day
In France they killed him. It was back in March,
The very night of the blizzard, too. Now if
He had stayed here we should have moved the tree.'
'And I should not have sat here. Everything
Would have been different. For it would have been
Another world.' 'Ay, and a better, though
If we could see all all might seem good.' Then
The lovers came out of the wood again:

The horses started and for the last time
I watched the clods crumble and topple over
After the ploughshare and the stumbling team.

Gone, Gone Again

Gone, gone again,
May, June, July,
And August gone,
Again gone by,

Not memorable
Save that I saw them go,
As past the empty quays
The rivers flow.

And now again,
In the harvest rain,
The Blenheim oranges
Fall grubby from the trees

As when I was young –
And when the lost one was here –
And when the war began
To turn young men to dung.

Look at the old house,
Outmoded, dignified,
Dark and untenanted,
With grass growing instead

Of the footsteps of life,
The friendliness, the strife;
In its beds have lain
Youth, love, age, and pain:

I am something like that;
Only I am not dead,
Still breathing and interested
In the house that is not dark:—

I am something like that:
Not one pane to reflect the sun,
For the schoolboys to throw at –
They have broken every one.

EDMUND BLUNDEN

Two Voices

'There's something in the air,' he said
  In the farm parlour cool and bare;
Plain words, which in his hearers bred
  A tumult, yet in silence there
All waited; wryly gay, he left the phrase,
Ordered the march, and bade us go our ways.

'We're going South, man'; as he spoke
  The howitzer with huge ping-bang
Racked the light hut; as thus he broke
  The death-news, bright the skylarks sang;
He took his riding-crop and humming went
Among the apple-trees all bloom and scent.

Now far withdraws the roaring night
  Which wrecked our flower after the first
Of those two voices; misty light
  Shrouds Thiepval Wood and all its worst;
But still 'There's something in the air' I hear,
And still 'We're going South, man,' deadly near.

Preparations for Victory

  My soul, dread not the pestilence that hags
  The valley; flinch not you, my body young,

At these great shouting smokes and snarling jags
Of fiery iron; as yet may not be flung
The dice that claims you. Manly move among
These ruins, and what you must do, do well;
Look, here are gardens, there mossed boughs are hung
With apples whose bright cheeks none might excel,
And there's a house as yet unshattered by a shell.

'I'll do my best,' the soul makes sad reply,
'And I will mark the yet unmurdered tree,
The tokens of dear homes that court the eye,
And yet I see them not as I would see.
Hovering between, a ghostly enemy.
Sickens the light, and poisoned, withered, wan,
The least defiled turns desperate to me.'
The body, poor unpitied Caliban,
Parches and sweats and grunts to win the name of Man.

Days or eternities like swelling waves
Surge on, and still we drudge in this dark maze;
The bombs and coils and cans by strings of slaves
Are borne to serve the coming day of days;
Pale sleep in slimy cellars scarce allays
With its brief blank the burden. Look, we lose;
The sky is gone, the lightless, drenching haze
Of rainstorm chills the bone; earth, air are foes,
The black fiend leaps brick-red as life's last picture goes.

Come On, My Lucky Lads

O rosy red, O torrent splendour
    Staining all the Orient gloom,
O celestial work of wonder –
    A million mornings in one bloom!

What, does the artist of creation
  Try some new plethora of flame,
For his eye's fresh fascination?
  Has the old cosmic fire grown tame?

In what subnatural strange awaking
  Is this body, which seems mine?
These feet towards that blood-burst making,
  These ears which thunder, these hands which twine

On grotesque iron? Icy-clear
  The air of a mortal day shocks sense,
My shaking men pant after me here.
  The acid vapours hovering dense,

The fury whizzing in dozens down,
  The clattering rafters, clods calcined,
The blood in the flints and the trackway brown –
  I see I am clothed and in my right mind;

The dawn but hangs behind the goal,
  What is that artist's joy to me?
Here limps poor Jock with a gash in the poll,
  His red blood now is the red I see,

The swooning white of him, and that red!
  These bombs in boxes, the craunch of shells,
The second-hand flitting round; ahead!
  It's plain we were born for this, naught else.

The Zonnebeke Road

Morning, if this late withered light can claim
Some kindred with that merry flame
Which the young day was wont to fling through space!
Agony stares from each grey face.

And yet the day is come; stand down! stand down!
Your hands unclasp from rifles while you can;
The frost has pierced them to the bended bone?
Why, see old Stevens there, that iron man,
Melting the ice to shave his grotesque chin!
Go ask him, shall we win?
I never liked this bay, some foolish fear
Caught me the first time that I came in here;
That dugout fallen in awakes, perhaps,
Some formless haunting of some corpse's chaps.
True, and wherever we have held the line,
There were such corners, seeming-saturnine
For no good cause.
                      Now where Haymarket starts,
That is no place for soldiers with weak hearts;
The minenwerfers have it to the inch.
Look, how the snow-dust whisks along the road
Piteous and silly; the stones themselves must flinch
In this east wind; the low sky like a load
Hangs over, a dead-weight. But what a pain
Must gnaw where its clay cheek
Crushes the shell-chopped trees that fang the plain –
The ice-bound throat gulps out a gargoyle shriek.
That wretched wire before the village line
Rattles like rusty brambles or dead bine,
And there the daylight oozes into dun;
Black pillars, those are trees where roadways run.
Even Ypres now would warm our souls; fond fool,
Our tour's but one night old, seven more to cool!
O screaming dumbness, O dull clashing death,
Shreds of dead grass and willows, homes and men,
Watch as you will, men clench their chattering teeth
And freeze you back with that one hope, disdain.

Vlamertinghe: Passing the Château, July, 1917

'And all her silken flanks with garlands drest' –
But we are coming to the sacrifice.
Must those have flowers who are not yet gone West?
May those have flowers who live with death and lice?
This must be the floweriest place
That earth allows; the queenly face
Of the proud mansion borrows grace for grace
Spite of those brute guns lowing at the skies.

Bold great daisies' golden lights,
Bubbling roses' pinks and whites –
Such a gay carpet! poppies by the million;
Such damask! such vermilion!
But if you ask me, mate, the choice of colour
Is scarcely right; this red should have been duller.

Third Ypres

Triumph! How strange, how strong had triumph come
On weary hate of foul and endless war
When from its grey gravecloths awoke anew
The summer day. Among the tumbled wreck
Of fascined lines and mounds the light was peering,
Half-smiling upon us, and our newfound pride;
The terror of the waiting night outlived,
The time too crowded for the heart to count
All the sharp cost in friends killed on the assault.
No hook of all the octopus had held us,
Here stood we trampling down the ancient tyrant.
So shouting dug we among the monstrous pits.
Amazing quiet fell upon the waste,
Quiet intolerable to those who felt
The hurrying batteries beyond the masking hills

For their new parley setting themselves in array
In crafty forms unmapped.
                                    No, these, smiled Faith,
Are dumb for the reason of their overthrow.
They move not back, they lie among the crews
Twisted and choked, they'll never speak again.
Only the copse where once might stand a shrine
Still clacked and suddenly hissed its bullets by.
The War would end, the Line was on the move,
And at a bound the impassable was passed.
We lay and waited with extravagant joy.

Now dulls the day and chills; comes there no word
From those who swept through our new lines to flood
The lines beyond? but little comes, and so
Sure as a runner time himself's accosted.
And the slow moments shake their heavy heads,
And croak, 'They're done, they'll none of them get
    through.
They're done, they've all died on the entanglements,
The wire stood up like an unplashed hedge and thorned
With giant spikes – and there they've paid the bill.'
Then comes the black assurance, then the sky's
Mute misery lapses into trickling rain,
That wreathes and swims and soon shuts in our world,
And those distorted guns, that lay past use,
Why – miracles not over! – all a-firing!
The rain's no cloak from their sharp eyes. And you,
Poor signaller, you I passed by this emplacement,
You whom I warned, poor daredevil, waving your flags,
Among this screeching I pass you again and shudder
At the lean green flies upon the red flesh madding.
Runner, stand by a second. Your message. – He's gone,
Falls on a knee, and his right hand uplifted
Claws his last message from his ghostly enemy,
Turns stone-like. Well I liked him, that young runner,

But there's no time for that. O now for the word
To order us flash from these drowning roaring traps
And even hurl upon that snarling wire?
Why are our guns so impotent?

                      The grey rain,
Steady as the sand in an hourglass on this day,
Where through the window the red lilac looks,
And all's so still, the chair's odd click is noise –
The rain is all heaven's answer, and with hearts
Past reckoning we are carried into night
And even sleep is nodding here and there.
The second night steals through the shrouding rain.
We in our numb thought crouching long have lost
The mockery triumph, and in every runner
Have urged the mind's eye see the triumph to come
The sweet relief, the straggling out of hell
Into whatever burrows may be given
For life's recall. Then the fierce destiny speaks.
This was the calm, we shall look back for this.
The hour is come; come, move to the relief!
Dizzy we pass the mule-strewn track where once
The ploughman whistled as he loosed his team;
And where he turned home-hungry on the road,
The leaning pollard marks us hungrier turning.
We crawl to save the remnant who have torn
Back from the tentacled wire, those whom no shell
Has charred into black carcasses – Relief!
They grate their teeth until we take their room,
And through the churn of moonless night and mud
And flaming burst and sour gas we are huddled
Into the ditches where they bawl sense awake,
And in a frenzy that none could reason calm
(Whimpering some, and calling on the dead),
They turn away: as in a dream they find
Strength in their feet to bear back that strange whim
Their body.

At the noon of the dreadful day
Our trench and death's is on a sudden stormed
With huge and shattering salvoes, the clay dances
In founts of clods around the concrete sties,
Where still the brain devises some last armour
To live out the poor limbs.
                    This wrath's oncoming
Found four of us together in a pillbox,
Skirting the abyss of madness with light phrases,
White and blinking, in false smiles grimacing.
The demon grins to see the game, a moment
Passes, and – still the drum-tap dongs my brain
To a whirring void – through the great breach above me
The light comes in with icy shock and the rain
Horribly drips. Doctor, talk, talk! if dead
Or stunned I know not; the stinking powdered concrete,
The lyddite turns me sick – my hair's all full
Of this smashed concrete. O, I'll drag you, friends,
Out of the sepulchre into the light of day,
For this is day, the pure and sacred day.
And while I squeak and gibber over you,
Look, from the wreck a score of field-mice nimble,
And tame and curious look about them; (these
Calmed me, on these depended my salvation).
There comes my sergeant, and by all the powers
The wire is holding to the right battalion,
And I can speak – but I myself first spoken
Hear a known voice now measured even to madness
Call me by name.
               'For God's sake send and help us,
Here in a gunpit, all headquarters done for,
Forty or more, the nine-inch came right through,
All splashed with arms and legs, and I myself
The only one not killed nor even wounded.
You'll send – God bless you!' The more monstrous fate
Shadows our own, the mind swoons doubly burdened,

Taught how for miles our anguish groans and bleeds,
A whole sweet countryside amuck with murder;
Each moment puffed into a year with death
Still wept the rain, roared guns,
Still swooped into the swamps of flesh and blood,
All to the drabness of uncreation sunk,
And all thought dwindled to a moan, Relieve!
But who with what command can now relieve
The dead men from that chaos, or my soul?

Gouzeaucourt: The Deceitful Calm

How unpurposed, how inconsequential
Seemed those southern lines when in the pallor
      Of the dying winter
      First we went there!

Grass thin-waving in the wind approached them,
Red roofs in the near view feigned survival,
      Lovely mockers, when we
      There took over.

There war's holiday seemed, nor though at known times
Gusts of flame and jingling steel descended
      On the bare tracks, would you
      Picture death there.

Snow or rime-frost made a solemn silence,
Bluish darkness wrapped in dangerous safety;
      Old hands thought of tidy
      Living-trenches!

There it was, my dear, that I departed,
Scarce a simpler traitor ever! There, too,
      Many of you soon paid for
      That false mildness.

La Quinque Rue

O road in dizzy moonlight bleak and blue,
With forlorn effigies of farms besprawled,
With trees bitterly bare or snapped in two,
Why riddle me thus – attracted and appalled?
For surely now the grounds both left and right
Are tilled, and scarless houses undismayed
Glow in the lustrous mercy of sweet night,
And one may hear the flute or fiddle played.
Why lead me then
Through the foul-gorged, the cemeterial fen
To fear sharp sentries? Why do dreadful rags
Fur these bulged banks, and feebly move to the wind?
That battered drum, say why it clacks and brags?
Another and another! what's behind?
How is it that these flints flame out fire's tongue,
Shrivelling my thought? these collapsed skeletons,
What are they, and these iron hunks among?
Why clink those spades, why glare these startling suns
And topple to the wet and crawling grass,
Where the shrill briars in taloned hedges twine?
What need of that stopped tread, that countersign?
O road, I know those muttering groups you pass,
I know your art of turning blood to glass;
But, I am told, to-night you safely shine
To trim roofs and cropped fields; the error's mine.

The Ancre at Hamel: Afterwards

Where tongues were loud and hearts were light
    I heard the Ancre flow;
Waking oft at the mid of night
    I heard the Ancre flow.

I heard it crying, that sad rill,
  Below the painful ridge
By the burnt unraftered mill
  And the relic of a bridge.

And could this sighing river seem
  To call me far away,
And its pale word dismiss as dream
  The voices of to-day?
The voices in the bright room chilled
  And that mourned on alone;
The silence of the full moon filled
  With that brook's troubling tone.

The struggling Ancre had no part
  In these new hours of mine,
And yet its stream ran through my heart;
  I heard it grieve and pine,
As if its rainy tortured blood
  Had swirled into my own,
When by its battered bank I stood
  And shared its wounded moan.

1916 seen from 1921

Tired with dull grief, grown old before my day,
I sit in solitude and only hear
Long silent laughters, murmurings of dismay,
The lost intensities of hope and fear;
In those old marshes yet the rifles lie,
On the thin breastwork flutter the grey rags,
The very books I read are there – and I
Dead as the men I loved, wait while life drags

Its wounded length from those sad streets of war
Into green places here, that were my own;
But now what once was mine is mine no more,
I seek such neighbours here and I find none.
With such strong gentleness and tireless will
Those ruined houses seared themselves in me,
Passionate I look for their dumb story still,
And the charred stub outspeaks the living tree.

I rise up at the singing of a bird
And scarcely knowing slink along the lane,
I dare not give a soul a look or word
Where all have homes and none's at home in vain:
Deep red the rose burned in the grim redoubt,
The self-sown wheat around was like a flood,
In the hot path the lizard lolled time out,
The saints in broken shrines were bright as blood.

Sweet Mary's shrine between the sycamores!
There we would go, my friend of friends and I,
And snatch long moments from the grudging wars,
Whose dark made light intense to see them by.
Shrewd bit the morning fog, the whining shots
Spun from the wrangling wire; then in warm swoon
The sun hushed all but the cool orchard plots,
We crept in the tall grass and slept till noon.

Report on Experience

I have been young, and now am not too old;
And I have seen the righteous forsaken,
His health, his honour and his quality taken.
    This is not what we were formerly told.

I have seen a green country, useful to the race,
Knocked silly with guns and mines, its villages vanished,

Even the last rat and last kestrel banished –
　　God bless us all, this was peculiar grace.

I knew Seraphina; Nature gave her hue,
Glance, sympathy, note, like one from Eden.
I saw her smile warp, heard her lyric deaden;
　　She turned to harlotry; – this I took to be new.

Say what you will, our God sees how they run.
These disillusions are His curious proving
That He loves humanity and will go on loving;
　　Over there are faith, life, virtue in the sun.

The Midnight Skaters

The hop-poles stand in cones,
　　The icy pond lurks under,
The pole-tops steeple to the thrones
　　Of stars, sound gulfs of wonder;
But not the tallest there, 'tis said,
Could fathom to this pond's black bed.

Then is not death at watch
　　Within those secret waters?
What wants he but to catch
　　Earth's heedless sons and daughters?
With but a crystal parapet
Between, he has his engines set.

Then on, blood shouts, on, on,
　　Twirl, wheel and whip above him,
Dance on this ball-floor thin and wan,
　　Use him as though you love him;
Court him, elude him, reel and pass,
And let him hate you through the glass.

To His Love

He's gone, and all our plans
  Are useless indeed.
We'll walk no more on Cotswold
  Where the sheep feed
  Quietly and take no heed.

His body that was so quick
  Is not as you
Knew it, on Severn river
  Under the blue
  Driving our small boat through.

You would not know him now . . .
  But still he died
Nobly, so cover him over
  With violets of pride
  Purple from Severn side.

Cover him, cover him soon!
  And with thick-set
Masses of memoried flowers –
  Hide that red wet
  Thing I must somehow forget.

The Silent One

Who died on the wires, and hung there, one of two –
Who for his hours of life had chattered through
Infinite lovely chatter of Bucks accent:
Yet faced unbroken wires; stepped over, and went
A noble fool, faithful to his stripes – and ended.
But I weak, hungry, and willing only for the chance
Of line – to fight in the line, lay down under unbroken
Wires, and saw the flashes and kept unshaken,
Till the politest voice – a finicking accent, said:
'Do you think you might crawl through, there: there's
    a hole'
Darkness, shot at: I smiled, as politely replied –
'I'm afraid not, Sir.' There was no hole no way to be
    seen
Nothing but chance of death, after tearing of clothes
Kept flat, and watched the darkness, hearing bullets
    whizzing –
And thought of music – and swore deep heart's deep
    oaths
(Polite to God) and retreated and came on again,
Again retreated – and a second time faced the screen.

The Bohemians

Certain people would not clean their buttons,
Nor polish buckles after latest fashions,
Preferred their hair long, putties comfortable,
Barely escaping hanging, indeed hardly able,
In Bridge and smoking without army cautions
Spending hours that sped like evil for quickness,
(While others burnished brasses, earned promotions)
These were those ones who jested in the trench,

While others argued of army ways, and wrenched
What little soul they had still further from shape,
And died off one by one, or became officers
Without the first of dream, the ghost of notions
Of ever becoming soldiers, or smart and neat,
Surprised as ever to find the army capable
Of sounding 'Lights out' to break a game of Bridge,
As to fear candles would set a barn alight.
In Artois or Picardy they lie – free of useless fashions.

War Books

What did they expect of our toil and extreme
Hunger – the perfect drawing of a heart's dream?
Did they look for a book of wrought art's perfection,
Who promised no reading, nor praise, nor publication?
Out of the heart's sickness the spirit wrote
For delight, or to escape hunger, or of war's worst anger,
When the guns died to silence and men would gather
    sense
Somehow together, and find this was life indeed,
And praise another's nobleness, or to Cotswold get hence.
There we wrote – Corbie Ridge – or in Gonnehem at rest.
Or Fauquissart or world's death songs, ever the best.
One made sorrows' praise passing the Church where
    silence
Opened for the long quivering strokes of the bell –
Another wrote all soldiers' praise, and of France and
    night's stars.
Served his guns, got immortality, and died well.
But Ypres played another trick with its danger on me,
Kept still the needing and loving of action body;
Gave no candles, and nearly killed me twice as well,

And no souvenirs though I risked my life in the stuck
    tanks,
Yet there was praise of Ypres, love came sweet in hospital
And old Flanders went under to long ages of plays
    thought in my pages.

Strange Hells

There are strange Hells within the minds War made
Not so often, not so humiliatingly afraid
As one would have expected – the racket and fear guns
    made.

One Hell the Gloucester soldiers they quite put out;
Their first bombardment, when in combined black shout
Of fury, guns aligned, they ducked low their heads
And sang with diaphragms fixed beyond all dreads,
That tin and stretched-wire tinkle, that blither of tune;
'Après la guerre fini' till Hell all had come down,
Twelve-inch, six-inch, and eighteen pounders hammering
    Hell's thunders.

Where are they now on State-doles, or showing shop
    patterns
Or walking town to town sore in borrowed tatterns
Or begged. Some civic routine one never learns.
The heart burns – but has to keep out of face how heart
    burns.

To Robert Nichols

(From Frise on the Somme in February 1917, in answer to
a letter, saying: 'I am just finishing my "Faun's Holiday".
I wish you were here to feed him with cherries.')

Here by a snowbound river
In scrapen holes we shiver,
And like old bitterns we
Boom to you plaintively:
Robert, how can I rhyme
Verses for your desire –
Sleek fauns and cherry-time,
Vague music and green trees,
Hot sun and gentle breeze,
England in June attire,
And life born young again,
For your gay goatish brute
Drunk with warm melody
Singing on beds of thyme
With red and rolling eye,
Waking with wanton lute
All the Devonian plain,
Lips dark with juicy stain,
Ears hung with bobbing fruit?
Why should I keep him time?
Why in this cold and rime,
Where even to dream is pain?
No, Robert, there's no reason:
Cherries are out of season,

Ice grips at branch and root,
And singing birds are mute.

Recalling War

Entrance and exit wounds are silvered clean,
The track aches only when the rain reminds.
The one-legged man forgets his leg of wood,
The one-armed man his jointed wooden arm.
The blinded man sees with his ears and hands
As much or more than once with both his eyes.
Their war was fought these twenty years ago
And now assumes the nature-look of time,
As when the morning traveller turns and views
His wild night-stumbling carved into a hill.

What, then, was war? No mere discord of flags
But an infection of the common sky
That sagged ominously upon the earth
Even when the season was the airiest May.
Down pressed the sky, and we, oppressed, thrust out
Boastful tongue, clenched fist and valiant yard.
Natural infirmities were out of mode,
For Death was young again: patron alone
Of healthy dying, premature fate-spasm.

Fear made fine bed-fellows. Sick with delight
At life's discovered transitoriness,
Our youth became all-flesh and waived the mind.
Never was such antiqueness of romance,
Such tasty honey oozing from the heart.
And old importances came swimming back –
Wine, meat, log-fires, a roof over the head,
A weapon at the thigh, surgeons at call.

Even there was a use again for God –
A word of rage in lack of meat, wine, fire,
In ache of wounds beyond all surgeoning.

War was return of earth to ugly earth,
War was foundering of sublimities,
Extinction of each happy art and faith
By which the world had still kept head in air.
Protesting logic or protesting love,
Until the unendurable moment struck –
The inward scream, the duty to run mad.

And we recall the merry ways of guns –
Nibbling the walls of factory and church
Like a child, piecrust; felling groves of trees
Like a child, dandelions with a switch!
Machine-guns rattle toy-like from a hill,
Down in a row the brave tin-soldiers fall:
A sight to be recalled in elder days
When learnedly the future we devote
To yet more boastful visions of despair.

SIEGFRIED SASSOON

A Working Party

Three hours ago he blundered up the trench,
Sliding and poising, groping with his boots;
Sometimes he tripped and lurched against the walls
With hands that pawed the sodden bags of chalk.
He couldn't see the man who walked in front;
Only he heard the drum and rattle of feet
Stepping along barred trench boards, often splashing
Wretchedly where the sludge was ankle-deep.

Voices would grunt 'Keep to your right – make way!'
When squeezing past some men from the front-line:
White faces peered, puffing a point of red;
Candles and braziers glinted through the chinks
And curtain-flaps of dug-outs; then the gloom
Swallowed his sense of sight; he stooped and swore
Because a sagging wire had caught his neck.

A flare went up; the shining whiteness spread
And flickered upward, showing nimble rats
And mounds of glimmering sand-bags, bleached with
    rain;
Then the slow silver moment died in dark.
The wind came posting by with chilly gusts
And buffeting at corners, piping thin.
And dreary through the crannies; rifle-shots
Would split and crack and sing along the night,
And shells came calmly through the drizzling air
To burst with hollow bang below the hill.

Three hours ago he stumbled up the trench;
Now he will never walk that road again:
He must be carried back, a jolting lump
Beyond all need of tenderness and care.

He was a young man with a meagre wife
And two small children in a Midland town;
He showed their photographs to all his mates,
And they considered him a decent chap
Who did his work and hadn't much to say,
And always laughed at other people's jokes
Because he hadn't any of his own.

That night when he was busy at his job
Of piling bags along the parapet,
He thought how slow time went, stamping his feet
And blowing on his fingers, pinched with cold.
He thought of getting back by half-past twelve,
And tot of rum to send him warm to sleep
In draughty dug-out frowsty with the fumes
Of coke, and full of snoring weary men.

He pushed another bag along the top,
Craning his body outward; then a flare
Gave one white glimpse of No Man's Land and wire,
And as he dropped his head the instant split
His startled life with lead, and all went out.

'The rank stench of those bodies haunts me still'

The rank stench of those bodies haunts me still,
And I remember things I'd best forget.
For now we've marched to a green, trenchless land
Twelve miles from battering guns: along the grass
Brown lines of tents are hives for snoring men;

Wide, radiant water sways the floating sky
Below dark, shivering trees. And living-clean
Comes back with thoughts of home and hours of sleep.

To-night I smell the battle; miles away
Gun-thunder leaps and thuds along the ridge;
The spouting shells dig pits in fields of death,
And wounded men, are moaning in the woods.
If any friend be there whom I have loved,
    speed
God (send) him safe to England with a gash.

It's sundown in the camp; some youngster laughs,
Lifting his mug and drinking health to all
       come
Who (came) unscathed from that unpitying waste: –
(Terror and ruin lurk behind his gaze.)
Another sits with tranquil, musing face,
Puffing his pipe and dreaming of the girl
         letter
Whose last scrawled (sheets) lies upon his knee.
The sunlight falls, low-ruddy from the west,
      heads; last week
Upon their (martial hair;) they might have died;
And now they stretch their limbs in tired content.

       Bosche has
One says 'The bloody (Bosches have) got the knock;
'And soon they'll crumple up and chuck their games.
'We've got the beggars on the run at last!'

Then I remembered someone that I'd seen
    a
Dead in (the) squalid, miserable ditch,
Heedless of toiling feet that trod him down.

He was a Prussian with a decent face,
Young, fresh, and pleasant, so I dare to say.

No doubt he loathed the war and longed for peace,
And cursed our souls because we'd killed his friends.

One night he yawned along a half-dug trench
Midnight; and then the British guns began
With heavy shrapnel bursting low, and 'hows'
Whistling to cut the wire with blinding din.
  He didn't move; the digging still went on;
Men stooped and shovelled; someone gave a grunt,
                                        sludge.
And moaned and died with agony in the (sand:)
Then the long hiss of shells lifted and stopped.

He stared into the gloom; a rocket curved,
                        (fretfully) angrily
And rifles rattled (sharply) on the left
Down by the wood, and there was noise of bombs.
  Then the damned English loomed in scrambling haste
Out of the dark and struggled through the wire,
And there were shouts and curses; someone screamed
And men began to (do) blunder down the trench
Without their rifles. It was time to go:
                                        some
He grabbed his coat; stood up, gulping (the) bread;
Then clutched his head and fell.
                        I found him there
In the gray morning when the place was held.
His face was in the mud; one arm flung out
As when he crumpled up; his sturdy legs
Were bent beneath his trunk; heels to the sky.
(dated) *July 1916*

The manuscript of this poem was given by Siegfried Sassoon to
the editor, in Sassoon's home, at approximately the beginning
of March 1965. It is written on four leaves of lined exercise-
book paper, in Sassoon's hand, together with corrections by
him, which we have tried to reproduce as nearly as possible.

All material in brackets was deleted by Sassoon. Versions out-
side brackets represent the poet's final emendations.

14. speed] send
17. come] came
21. letter] sheets
23. heads; last week] martial hair
25. Bosche has] Bosches have
29. a] the
41. sludge] sand:
44. angrily] (a) sharply
              (b) fretfully
49. (do) *sic*
51. some] the

The Death-Bed

He drowsed and was aware of silence heaped
Round him, unshaken as the steadfast walls;
Aqueous like floating rays of amber light,
Soaring and quivering in the wings of sleep.
Silence and safety; and his mortal shore
Lipped by the inward, moonless waves of death.

Someone was holding water to his mouth.
He swallowed, unresisting; moaned and dropped
Through crimson gloom to darkness; and forgot
The opiate throb and ache that was his wound.
  Water – calm, sliding green above the weir.
  Water – a sky-lit alley for his boat,
  Bird-voiced, and bordered with reflected flowers
  And shaken hues of summer; drifting down,
  He dipped contented oars, and sighed, and slept.

Night, with a gust of wind, was in the ward,
Blowing the curtain to a glimmering curve.
Night. He was blind; he could not see the stars

Glinting among the wraiths of wandering cloud;
Queer blots of colour, purple, scarlet, green,
Flickered and faded in his drowning eyes.

Rain – he could hear it rustling through the dark;
Fragrance and passionless music woven as one;
Warm rain on drooping roses; pattering showers
That soak the woods; not the harsh rain that sweeps
Behind the thunder, but a trickling peace,
Gently and slowly washing life away.

He stirred, shifting his body; then the pain
Leapt like a prowling beast, and gripped and tore
His groping dreams with grinding claws and fangs.
But someone was beside him; soon he lay
Shuddering because that evil thing had passed.
And death, who'd stepped toward him, paused and
stared.

Light many lamps and gather round his bed.
Lend him your eyes, warm blood, and will to live.
Speak to him; rouse him; you may save him yet.
He's young; he hated War; how should he die
When cruel old campaigners win safe through?

But death replied: 'I choose him.' So he went,
And there was silence in the summer night;
Silence and safety; and the veils of sleep.
Then, far away, the thudding of the guns.

Prelude: The Troops

Dim, gradual thinning of the shapeless gloom
Shudders to drizzling daybreak that reveals
Disconsolate men who stamp their sodden boots
And turn dulled, sunken faces to the sky

Haggard and hopeless. They, who have beaten down
The stale despair of night, must now renew
Their desolation in the truce of dawn,
Murdering the livid hours that grope for peace.

Yet these, who cling to life with stubborn hands,
Can grin through storms of death and find a gap
In the clawed, cruel tangles of his defence.
They march from safety, and the bird-sung joy
Of grass-green thickets, to the land where all
Is ruin, and nothing blossoms but the sky
That hastens over them where they endure
Sad, smoking, flat horizons, reeking woods,
And foundered trench-lines volleying doom for doom.

O my brave brown companions, when your souls
Flock silently away, and the eyeless dead
Shame the wild beast of battle on the ridge,
Death will stand grieving in that field of war
Since your unvanquished hardihood is spent.
And through some mooned Valhalla there will pass
Battalions and battalions, scarred from hell;
The unreturning army that was youth;
The legions who have suffered and are dust.

Counter-Attack

We'd gained our first objective hours before
While dawn broke like a face with blinking eyes,
Pallid, unshaved and thirsty, blind with smoke.
Things seemed all right at first. We held their line,
With bombers posted, Lewis guns well placed,
And clink of shovels deepening the shallow trench.
    The place was rotten with dead; green clumsy legs

High-booted, sprawled and grovelled along the saps
And trunks, face downward, in the sucking mud,
Wallowed like trodden sand-bags loosely filled;
And naked sodden buttocks, mats of hair,
Bulged, clotted heads slept in the plastering slime.
And then the rain began, – the jolly old rain!

A yawning soldier knelt against the bank,
Staring across the morning blear with fog;
He wondered when the Allemands would get busy;
And then, of course, they started with five-nines
Traversing, sure as fate, and never a dud.
Mute in the clamour of shells he watched them burst
Spouting dark earth and wire with gusts from hell,
While posturing giants dissolved in drifts of smoke.
He crouched and flinched, dizzy with galloping fear,
Sick for escape, – loathing the strangled horror
And butchered, frantic gestures of the dead.

An officer came blundering down the trench:
'Stand-to and man the fire-step!' On he went . . .
Gasping and bawling, 'Fire-step . . . counter-attack!'

Then the haze lifted. Bombing on the right
Down the old sap: machine-guns on the left;
And stumbling figures looming out in front.
'O Christ, they're coming at us!' Bullets spat,
And he remembered his rifle . . . rapid fire . . .
And started blazing wildly . . . then a bang
Crumpled and spun him sideways, knocked him out
To grunt and wriggle: none heeded him; he choked
And fought the flapping veils of smothering gloom,
Lost in a blurred confusion of yells and groans . . .
Down, and down, and down, he sank and drowned,
Bleeding to death. The counter-attack had failed.

Base Details

If I were fierce, and bald, and short of breath,
   I'd live with scarlet Majors at the Base,
And speed glum heroes up the line to death.
   You'd see me with my puffy petulant face,
Guzzling and gulping in the best hotel,
   Reading the Roll of Honour. 'Poor young chap,'
I'd say – 'I used to know his father well;
   Yes, we've lost heavily in this last scrap.'
And when the war is done and youth stone dead,
I'd toddle safely home and die – in bed.

Lamentations

I found him in the guard-room at the Base.
From the blind darkness I had heard his crying
And blundered in. With puzzled, patient face
A sergeant watched him; it was no good trying
To stop it; for he howled and beat his chest.
And, all because his brother had gone west,
Raved at the bleeding war; his rampant grief
Moaned, shouted, sobbed, and choked, while he was
   kneeling
Half-naked on the floor. In my belief
Such men have lost all patriotic feeling.

Does it Matter?

Does it matter? – losing your legs? . . .
For people will always be kind,
And you need not show that you mind

When the others come in after hunting
To gobble their muffins and eggs.

Does it matter? – losing your sight? . . .
There's such splendid work for the blind;
And people will always be kind,
As you sit on the terrace remembering
And turning your face to the light.

Do they matter? – those dreams from the pit? . . .
You can drink and forget and be glad,
And people won't say that you're mad;
For they'll know you've fought for your country
And no one will worry a bit.

Glory of Women

You love us when we're heroes, home on leave,
Or wounded in a mentionable place.
You worship decorations; you believe
That chivalry redeems the war's disgrace.
You make us shells. You listen with delight,
By tales of dirt and danger fondly thrilled.
You crown our distant ardours while we fight,
And mourn our laurelled memories when we're killed.
You can't believe that British troops 'retire'
When hell's last horror breaks them, and they run,
Trampling the terrible corpses – blind with blood.
    O German mother dreaming by the fire,
      While you are knitting socks to send your son
      His face is trodden deeper in the mud.

Repression of War Experience

Now light the candles; one; two; there's a moth;
What silly beggars they are to blunder in
And scorch their wings with glory, liquid flame –
No, no, not that, – it's bad to think of war,
When thoughts you've gagged all day come back to
    scare you;
And it's been proved that soldiers don't go mad
Unless they lose control of ugly thoughts
That drive them out to jabber among the trees.

Now light your pipe; look, what a steady hand.
Draw a deep breath; stop thinking; count fifteen,
And you're as right as rain . . .
                        Why won't it rain? . . .
I wish there'd be a thunder-storm to-night,
With bucketsful of water to sluice the dark,
And make the roses hang their dripping heads.
Books; what a jolly company they are,
Standing so quiet and patient on their shelves,
Dressed in dim brown, and black, and white, and green,
And every kind of colour. Which will you read?
Come on; O *do* read something; they're so wise.
I tell you all the wisdom of the world
Is waiting for you on those shelves; and yet
You sit and gnaw your nails, and let your pipe out,
And listen to the silence: on the ceiling
There's one big, dizzy moth that bumps and flutters;
And in the breathless air outside the house
The garden waits for something that delays.
There must be crowds of ghosts among the trees, –
Not people killed in battle, – they're in France, –
But horrible shapes in shrouds – old men who died
Slow, natural deaths, – old men with ugly souls,
Who wore their bodies out with nasty sins.

You're quiet and peaceful, summering safe at home;
You'd never think there was a bloody war on! . . .
O yes, you would . . . why, you can hear the guns.
Hark! Thud, thud, thud, – quite soft . . . they never
    cease –
Those whispering guns – O Christ, I want to go out
And screech at them to stop – I'm going crazy;
I'm going stark, staring mad because of the guns.

Epitaphs of the War (1914–18)

A Servant

We were together since the War began.
He was my servant – and the better man.

A Son

My son was killed while laughing at some jest. I would
I knew
What it was, and it might serve me in a time when jests
are few.

The Coward

I could not look on Death, which being known,
Men led me to him, blindfold and alone.

Pelicans in the Wilderness (*A Grave near Halfa*)

The blown sand heaps on me, that none may learn
Where I am laid for whom my children grieve . . .
O wings that beat at dawning, ye return
Out of the desert to your young at eve!

The Refined Man

I was of delicate mind. I stepped aside for my needs,
Disdaining the common office. I was seen from afar
and killed . . .

How is this matter for mirth? Let each man be judged
    by his deeds.
I have paid my price to live with myself on the terms
    that I willed.

Common Form

If any question why we died,
Tell them, because our fathers lied.

A Drifter off Tarentum

He from the wind-bitten north with ship and
    companions descended.
  Searching for eggs of death spawned by invisible
    hulls.
Many he found and drew forth. Of a sudden the fishery
    ended
  In flame and a clamorous breath not new to the
    eye-pecking gulls.

Gethsemane (1914–18)

The Garden called Gethsemane
  In Picardy it was,
And there the people came to see
  The English soldiers pass.

We used to pass – we used to pass
  Or halt, as it might be,
And ship our masks in case of gas
  Beyond Gethsemane.

The Garden called Gethsemane,
  It held a pretty lass,

But all the time she talked to me
  I prayed my cup might pass.
The officer sat on the chair,
  The men lay on the grass,
And all the time we halted there
  I prayed my cup might pass.

It didn't pass – it didn't pass –
  It didn't pass from me.
I drank it when we met the gas
  Beyond Gethsemane!

The Soldier Addresses his Body

I shall be mad if you get smashed about,
we've had good times together, you and I;
although you groused a bit when luck was out,
say a girl turned us down, or we went dry.

But there's a world of things we haven't done,
countries not seen, where people do strange things;
eat fish alive, and mimic in the sun
the solemn gestures of their stone-grey kings.

I've heard of forests that are dim at noon
where snakes and creepers wrestle all day long;
where vivid beasts grow pale with the full moon,
gibber and cry, and wail a mad old song;

because at the full moon the Hippogriff
with crinkled ivory snout and agate feet,
with his green eye will glare them cold and stiff
for the coward Wyvern to come down and eat.

Vodka and kvass, and bitter mountain wines
we've never drunk; nor snatched the bursting grapes
to pelt slim girls among Sicilian vines,
who'd flicker through the leaves, faint frolic shapes.

Yes, there's a world of things we've never done,
but it's a sweat to knock them into rhyme,
let's have a drink, and give the cards a run
and leave dull verse to the dull peaceful time.

Winter Warfare

Colonel Cold strode up the Line
   (tabs of rime and spurs of ice);
stiffened all that met his glare:
   horses, men, and lice.

Visited a forward post,
   left them burning, ear to foot;
fingers stuck to biting steel,
   toes to frozen boot.

Stalked on into No Man's Land,
   turned the wire to fleecy wool,
iron stakes to sugar sticks
   snapping at a pull.

Those who watched with hoary eyes
   saw two figures gleaming there;
Hauptmann Kälte, Colonel Cold,
   gaunt in the grey air.

Stiffly, tinkling spurs they moved,
   glassy-eyed, with glinting heel
stabbing those who lingered there
   torn by screaming steel.

'my sweet old etcetera'

my sweet old etcetera
aunt lucy during the recent

war could and what
is more did tell you just
what everybody was fighting

for,
my sister

isabel created hundreds
(and
hundreds) of socks not to
mention shirts fleaproof earwarmers

etcetera wristers etcetera, my
mother hoped that

i would die etcetera
bravely of course my father used
to become hoarse talking about how it was
a privilege and if only he
could meanwhile my

self etcetera lay quietly
in the deep mud et

cetera
(dreaming,
et
     cetera, of
Your smile
eyes knees and of your Etcetera)

RICHARD ALDINGTON

Field Manoeuvres

Outpost Duty

The long autumn grass under my body
Soaks my clothes with its dew;
Where my knees press into the ground
I can feel the damp earth.

In my nostrils is the smell of the crushed grass,
Wet pine-cones and bark.

Through the great bronze pine trunks
Glitters a silver segment of road.
Interminable squadrons of silver and blue horses
Pace in long ranks the blank fields of heaven.

There is no sound;
The wind hisses gently through the pine needles;
The flutter of a finch's wings about my head
Is like distant thunder,
And the shrill cry of a mosquito
Sounds loud and close.

I am 'to fire at the enemy column
After it has passed' –
But my obsolete rifle, loaded with 'blank',
Lies untouched before me,
My spirit follows after the gliding clouds,
And my lips murmur of the mother of beauty
Standing breast-high, in golden broom
Among the blue pine-woods!

In the Trenches

1

Not that we are weary,
Not that we fear,
Not that we are lonely
Though never alone –
Not these, not these destroy us;
But that each rush and crash
Of mortar and shell,
Each cruel bitter shriek of bullet
That tears the wind like a blade,
Each wound on the breast of earth,
Of Demeter, our Mother,
Wound us also,
Sever and rend the fine fabric
Of the wings of our frail souls,
Scatter into dust the bright wings
Of Psyche!

2

Impotent,
How impotent is all this clamour,
This destruction and contest . . .
Night after night comes the moon
Haughty and perfect;
Night after night the Pleiades sing
And Orion swings his belt across the sky.
Night after night the frost
Crumbles the hard earth.

Soon the spring will drop flowers
And patient creeping stalk and leaf
Along these barren lines
Where the huge rats scuttle
And the hawk shrieks to the carrion crow.

Trench Idyll

We sat together in the trench,
He on a lump of frozen earth
Blown in the night before,
I on an unexploded shell;
And smoked and talked, like exiles,
Of how pleasant London was,
Its women, restaurants, night clubs, theatres,
How at that very hour
The taxi-cabs were taking folk to dine . . .
Then we sat silent for a while
As a machine-gun swept the parapet.

He said:
'I've been here on and off two years
And seen only one man killed'.

'That's odd.'

'The bullet hit him in the throat;
He fell in a heap on the fire-step,
And called out "My God! *dead!*"'

'Good Lord, how terrible!'

'Well, as to that, the nastiest job I've had
Was last year on this very front
Taking the discs at night from men
Who'd hung for six months on the wire
Just over there.
The worst of all was
They fell to pieces at a touch.
Thank God we couldn't see their faces;
They had gas helmets on . . .'

I shivered;
'It's rather cold here, sir, suppose we move?'

Resentment

Why should you try to crush me?
Am I so Christ-like?

You beat against me,
Immense waves, filthy with refuse.
I am the last upright of a smashed breakwater
But you shall not crush me
Though you bury me in foaming slime
And hiss your hatred about me.

You break over me, cover me;
I shudder at the contact;
Yet I pierce through you
And stand up, torn, dripping, shaken,
But whole and fierce.

FORD MADOX FORD

From 'Antwerp'

VI

This is Charing Cross;
It is midnight;
There is a great crowd
And no light.
A great crowd, all black that hardly whispers aloud.
Surely, that is a dead woman – a dead mother!
She has a dead face;
She is dressed all in black;
She wanders to the bookstall and back,
At the back of the crowd;
And back again and again back,
She sways and wanders.

This is Charing Cross;
It is one o'clock.
There is still a great cloud, and very little light;
Immense shafts of shadows over the black crowd
That hardly whispers aloud . . .
And now! . . . That is another dead mother,
And there is another and another and another . . .
And little children, all in black,
All with dead faces, waiting in all the waiting-places,
Wandering from the doors of the waiting-room
In the dim gloom.

These are the women of Flanders.
They await the lost.

They await the lost that shall never leave the dock;
They await the lost that shall never again come by the
  train
To the embraces of all these women with dead faces;
They await the lost who lie dead in trench and barrier
  and foss,
In the dark of the night.
This is Charing Cross; it is past one of the clock;
There is very little light.

There is so much pain.

That Exploit of Yours

I meet two soldiers sometimes here in Hell
The one, with a tear in the seat of his red pantaloons
Was stuck by a pitchfork,
Climbing a wall to steal apples.

The second has a seeming silver helmet,
Having died from the fall of his horse on some tram-lines
In Dortmund.

These two
Meeting in the vaulted and vaporous caverns of Hell
Exclaim always in identical tones:
'I at least have done my duty to Society and the
  Fatherland!'
It is strange how the cliché prevails . . .
For I will bet my hat that you who sent me here to Hell
Are saying the selfsame words at this very moment
Concerning that exploit of yours.

Lament

The young men of the world
Are condemned to death.
They have been called up to die
For the crime of their fathers.

The young men of the world,
The growing, the ripening fruit,
Have been torn from their branches,
While the memory of the blossom
Is sweet in women's hearts;
They have been cast for a cruel purpose
Into the mashing-press and furnace.

The young men of the world
Look into each other's eyes,
And read there the same words:
Not yet! Not yet!
But soon perhaps, and perhaps certain.

The young men of the world
No longer possess the road:
The road possesses them.
They no longer inherit the earth:
The earth inherits them.
They are no longer the masters of fire:
Fire is their master;
They serve him, he destroys them.
They no longer rule the waters:

The genius of the seas
Has invented a new monster,
And they fly from its teeth.
They no longer breathe freely:
The genius of the air
Has contrived a new terror
That rends them into pieces.

The young men of the world
Are encompassed with death
He is all about them
In a circle of fire and bayonets.

Weep, weep, o women,
And old men break your hearts.

T. E. HULME

Trenches: St Eloi

Over the flat slope of St Eloi
A wide wall of sand bags.
Night,
In the silence desultory men
Pottering over small fires, cleaning their mess-tins:
To and fro, from the lines,
Men walk as on Piccadilly,
Making paths in the dark,
Through scattered dead horses,
Over a dead Belgian's belly.

The Germans have rockets. The English have no
 rockets.
Behind the line, cannon, hidden, lying back miles.
Before the line, chaos:

My mind is a corridor. The minds about me are
 corridors.
Nothing suggests itself. There is nothing to do but
 keep on.

(Abbreviated from the conversation of Mr T.E.H.)

The Happy Warrior

His wild heart beats with painful sobs
his strain'd hands clench an ice-cold rifle
his aching jaws grip a hot parch'd tongue
his wide eyes search unconsciously.

He cannot shriek.

Bloody saliva
dribbles down his shapeless jacket.

I saw him stab
and stab again
a well-killed Boche.

This is the happy warrior,
this is he . . .

The End of a War

In former days we used to look at life, and sometimes from a
distance, at death, and still further removed from us, at eternity.
Today it is from afar that we look at life, death is near us, and
perhaps nearer still is eternity.

JEAN BOUVIER, a French subaltern, February 1916

Argument

In the early days of November 1918, the Allied Forces had
for some days been advancing in pursuit of the retreating

German Army. The advance was being carried out according to a schedule. Each division was given a line to which it must attain before nightfall; and this meant that each battalion in a division had to reach a certain point by a certain time. The schedule was in general being well adhered to, but the opposition encountered varied considerably at different points.

On November 10th, a certain English Battalion had been continuously harassed by machine-gun fire, and late in the afternoon was still far from its objective. Advancing under cover, it reached the edge of a plantation from which stretched a wide open space of cultivated land, with a village in front about 500 yards away. The officer in charge of the scouts was sent ahead with a corporal and two men to reconnoitre, and this little party reached the outskirts of the village without observing any signs of occupation. At the entrance of the village, propped against a tree, they found a German officer, wounded severely in the thigh. He was quite conscious and looked up calmly as Lieut. S—— approached him. He spoke English, and when questioned, intimated that the village had been evacuated by the Germans two hours ago.

Thereupon Lieut. S—— signalled back to the battalion, who then advanced along the road in marching formation. It was nearly dusk when they reached the small *place* in front of the church, and there they were halted. Immediately from several points, but chiefly from the tower of the church, a number of machine-guns opened fire on the massed men. A wild cry went up, and the men fled in rage and terror to the shelter of the houses, leaving a hundred of their companions and five officers dead or dying on the pavement. In the houses and the church they routed out the ambushed Germans and mercilessly bayoneted them.

The corporal who had been with Lieut. S—— ran to the entrance of the village, to settle with the wounded officer who had betrayed them. The German seemed to be expecting him; his face did not flinch as the bayonet descended.

When the wounded had been attended to, and the dead gathered together, the remaining men retired to the schoolhouse to rest for the night. The officers then went to the château of the village, and there in a gardener's cottage, searching for fuel, the corporal already mentioned found the naked body of a young girl. Both legs were severed, and one severed arm was found in another room. The body itself was covered with bayonet wounds. When the discovery was reported to Lieut. S——, he went to verify the strange crime, but there was nothing to be done; he was, moreover, sick and tired. He found a bed in another cottage near the château, where some old peasants were still cowering behind a screen. He fell into a deep sleep, and did not wake until the next morning, the 11th of November, 1918.

Meditation of a Dying German Officer

Ich sterbe . . . Life ebbs with an easy flow
and I've no anguish now. This failing light
is the world's light: it dies like a lamp
flickering for want of oil. When the last jump comes
and the axe-head blackness slips through flesh
that welcomes it with open but unquivering lips
then I shall be one with the Unknown
this Nothing which Heinrich made his argument
for God's existence: a concept beyond the mind's reach.
But why embody the Unknown: why give to God
anything but essence, intangible, invisible, inert?
The world is full of solid creatures – these
are the mind's material, these we must mould
into images, idols to worship and obey:

The Father and the Flag, and the wide Empire
of our creative hands. I have seen
the heart of Europe send its beating blood
like a blush over the world's pallid sphere
calling it to one life, one order and one living.
For that dream I've given my life and to the last
fought its listless enemies. Now Chaos intervenes
and I leave not gladly but with harsh disdain
a world too strong in folly for the bliss of dreams.

I fought with gladness. When others cursed the day
this stress was loosed
and men were driven into camps, to follow
with wonder, woe, or base delirium
the voiceless yet incessant surge
then I exulted: but with not more
than a nostril's distension, an eager eye
and fast untiring step.
                                   The first week
I crossed the Fatherland, to take my place
in the swift-wing'd swoop that all but ended
the assay in one wild and agile venture.
I was blooded then, but the wound
seared in the burning circlet of my spirit
served only to temper courage
with scorn of action's outcome.
Blooded but not beaten I left the ranks
to be a leader. Four years
I have lived in the ecstasy of battle.
The throbbing of guns, growing yearly,
has been drum music to my ears
the crash of shells the thrill of cymbals
bayonets fiddlers' bows and the crack of rifles
plucked harp strings. Now the silence
is unholy. Death has no deeper horror
than diminishing sound – ears that strain

for the melody of action, hear
only the empty silence of retreating life.
Darkness will be kinder.

                      I die –

But still I hear a distant gunfire, stirring in my ear
like a weary humming nerve. I will cling to that sound
and on its widening wave
lapse into eternity. Heinrich, are you near?
Best friend, but false to my faith
would you die doubtfully with so calm a gaze?
Mind above battles, does your heart resign
love of the Fatherland in this hour of woe?
No drum will beat in your dying ears, and your God
will meet you with a cold embrace.
The void is icy: your Abstraction
freezes the blood at death: no calm
bound in such a barren law. The bond between
two human hearts is richer. Love can seal
the anguish'd ventricles with subtle fire
and make life end in peace, in love
the love we shared in all this strife.
Heinrich, your God has not this power, or he would heal
the world's wounds and create the empire
now left in the defeated hands of men.

At Valenciennes I saw you turn
swiftly into an open church. I followed
stood in the shadow of the aisle
and watched you pray. My impulse then
was to meet you in the porch and test
my smile against your smile, my peace against yours
and from your abashment pluck a wilder hope.
But the impulse died in the act: your face was blank
drained of sorrow as of joy, and I was dumb
before renunciation's subtler calm.
I let you pass, and into the world

went to deny my sight, to seal my lips
against the witness of your humble faith.
For my faith was action: is action now!
In death I triumph with a deed
and prove my faith against your passive ghost.

Faith in self comes first, from self we build
the web of friendship, from friends to confederates
and so to the State. This web has a weft
in the land we live in, a town, a hill
all that the living eyes traverse. There are lights
given by the tongue we speak, the songs we sing,
the music and the magic of our Fatherland.
This is a tangible trust. To make it secure
against the tempests of inferior minds
to build it in our blood, to make our lives
a tribute to its beauty – there is no higher aim.
This good achieved, then to God we turn
for a crown on our perfection: God we create
in the end of action, not in dreams.

God dies in this dying light. The mists receive
my spent spirit: there is no one to hear
my last wish. Already my thoughts
rebound in a tenement whose doors
are shut: strange muscles clench my jaws
these limbs are numb. I cannot lift
a finger to my will. But the mind
rises like a crystal sphere above the rigid wreck
is poised there, perhaps to fall into the void
still dreaming of an Empire of the West.
And so still feels no fear! Mind triumphs over flesh
ordering the body's action in direst danger.
Courage is not born in men, but born of love
love of life and love of giving, love
of this hour of death, which all love seeks.

I die, but death was destined. My life was given
my death ordained when first my hand
held naked weapons in this war. The rest
has been a waiting for this final hour.
In such a glory I could not always live.

My brow falls like a shutter of lead, clashes
on the clench'd jaw. The curtain of flesh
is wreathed about these rigid lines
in folds that have the easy notion of a smile.
So let them kiss earth and acid corruption:
extinction of the clod. The bubble is free
to expand to the world's confines or to break
against the pricking stars. The last lights shine
across its perfect crystal: rare ethereal glimmer
of mind's own intensity. Above the clod
all things are clear, and what is left
is petulant scorn, implanted passions,
everything not tensely ideal. Blind emotions
wreck the image with their blundering wings.
Mind must define before the heart intrigues.

Last light above the world, wavering in the darkest
void of Nothing – how still and tenuous
no music of the spheres – and so break with a sigh
against the ultimate
shores of this world
so finite
so small
Nichts

*Dialogue between the Body and the Soul of the
Murdered Girl*

BODY

I speak not from my pallid lips
but from these wounds.

SOUL

Red lips that cannot tell
a credible tale.

BODY

In a world of martyr'd men
these lips renounce their ravage:
The wounds of France
roused their fresh and fluid voices.

SOUL

War has victims beyond the bands
bonded to slaughter. War moves with armoured wheels
across the quivering flesh and patient limbs
of all life's labile fronds.

BODY

France was the garden I lived in.
Amid these trees, these fields, petals fell
flesh to flesh; I was a wilder flower.

SOUL

Open and innocent. So is the heart
laid virgin to my choice. I filled
your vacant ventricles with dreams
with immortal hopes and aspirations that exalt
the flesh to passion, to love and hate.
Child-radiance then is clouded, the light

that floods the mind is hot with blood
pulse beats to the vibrant battle-cry
the limbs are burnt with action.

BODY

The heart had not lost its innocence so soon
but for the coming of that day when men
speaking a strange tongue, wearing strange clothes
armed, flashing with harness and spurs
carrying rifles, lances or spears
followed by rumbling waggons, shrouded guns
passed through the village in endless procession
swift, grim, scornful, exulting.

SOUL

You had not lost your innocence so soon
but for the going of men from the village
your father gone, your brother
only the old left, and the very young
the women sad, the houses shuttered
suspense of school, even of play
the eager search for news, the air
of universal doubt, and then the knowledge
that the wavering line of battle now was fixed
beyond this home. The soil was tilled
for visionary hate.

BODY

Four years was time enough
for such a seedling hate to grow
sullen, close, intent;
To wait and wonder
but to abate
no fervour in the slow passage of despair.

SOUL

The mind grew tense.

BODY

My wild flesh was caught
in the cog and gear of hate.

SOUL

I lay coiled, the spring
of all your intricate design.

BODY

You served me well. But still I swear
Christ was my only King.

SOUL

France was your Motherland:
To her you gave your life and limbs.

BODY

I gave these hands and gave these arms
I gave my head of ravelled hair.

SOUL

You gave your sweet round breasts
like Agatha who was your Saint.

BODY

Mary Aegyptiaca
is the pattern of my greatest loss.

SOUL

To whom in nakedness and want
God sent a holy man.
Who clothed her, shrived her, gave her peace
before her spirit left the earth.

BODY

My sacrifice was made to gain
the secrets of these hostile men.

SOUL

I hover round your fameless features
barred from Heaven by light electric.

BODY

All men who find these mauled remains
will pray to Mary for your swift release.

SOUL

The cry that left your dying lips
was heard by God.

BODY

I died for France.

SOUL

A bright mantle fell across your bleeding limbs.
Your face averted shone with sacred fire.
So be content. In this war
many men have perished not bless'd
with faith in a cause, a country or a God
not less martyrs than Herod's Victims, Ursula's Virgins
or any mass'd innocents massacred.

BODY

Such men give themselves not to their God but to their
    fate
die thinking the face of God not love but hate.

SOUL

Those who die for a cause die comforted and coy;
believing their cause God's cause they die with joy.

Meditation of the Waking English Officer

I wake: I am alive: there is a bell
sounding with the dream's retreating surf
O catch the lacey hem dissolv'd in light
that creeps along the healing tendrils of a mind
still drugg'd with sleep. Why must my day
kill my dreams? Days of hate. But yes a bell
beats really on this air, a mad bell.
The peasants stir behind that screen.
Listen: they mutter now: they sing
in their old crackt voices, intone
a litany. There are no guns
only these voices of thanksgiving. Can it be?
Yes yes yes: it is peace, peace!
The world is very still, and I am alive!
Alive, alive, alive . . .
O limbs, your white radiance
no longer to stand against bloody shot
this heart secure, to live and worship
to go God's way, to grow in faith
to fight with and not against the will!
That day has come at last! Suspended life
renews its rhythmic beat. I live!
Now can I love and strive, as I have dreamt.

Lie still, and let this litany
of simple voices and the jubilant bell
ease rebirth. First there are the dead to bury
O God, the dead. How can God's bell
ring out from that unholy ambush?
That tower of death! In excess of horror
war died. The nerve was broken
fray'd men fought obscenely then: there was no fair joy
no glory in the strife, no blessed wrath.

Man's mind cannot excel
mechanic might except in savage sin.
Our broken bodies oiled the engines: mind was grit.

Shall I regret my pact? Envy that friend
who risked ignominy, insult, gaol
rather than stain his hands with human blood?
And left his fellow men. Such lonely pride
was never mine. I answered no call
there was no call to answer. I felt no hate
only the anguish of an unknown fate
a shot, a cry: then armies on the move
the sudden lull in daily life
all eyes wide with wonder, past surprise:
our felt dependence on a ruling few:
the world madness: the wild plunge:
the avalanche and I myself a twig
torn from its mother soil
and to the chaos rendered.
                              Listless
I felt the storm about me; its force
too strong to beat against; in its swirl
I spread my sapling arms, toss'd on its swell
I rose, I ran, I down the dark world sped
till death fell round me like a rain of steel
and hope and faith and love coiled in my inmost cell.

Often in the weariness of watching
warding weary men, pitch'd against
the unmeaning blackness of the night, the wet fog,
the enemy blanketed in mystery, often
I have questioned my life's inconstant drift;
God not real, hate not real, the hearts of men
insentient engines pumping blood
into a spongy mass that cannot move
above the indignity of inflicted death:
the only answer this: the infinite is all

and I, a finite speck, no essence even
of the life that falls like dew
from the spirit breathed on the fine edge
of matter, perhaps only that edge
a ridge between eternal death and life eternal
a moment of time, temporal.
The universe swaying between Nothing and Being
and life faltering like a clock's tick
between a pendulum's coming and going.
The individual lost: seventy years
seventy minutes, have no meaning.
Let death, I cried, come from the forward guns
let death come this moment, swift and crackling
tick-tock, tick-tock – moments that pass
not reckoned in the infinite.

Then I have said: all is that must be.
There is no volition, even prayer
dies on lips compress'd in fear.
Where all must be, there is no God
for God can only be the God of prayer
an infinitely kind Father whose will
can mould the world, who can
in answer to my prayer, mould me.
But whilst I cannot pray, I can't believe
but in this frame of machine necessity
must renounce not only God, but self.
For what is the self without God?
A moment not reckoned in the infinite.
My soul is less than nothing, lost,
unless in this life it can build
a bridge to life eternal.

In a warm room, by the flickering fire
in friendly debate, in some remote
shelter'd existence, even in the hermit's cell
easy it is to believe in God: extend the self

to communion with the infinite, the eternal.
But haggard in the face of death
deprived of all earthly comfort, all hope of life,
the soul a distill'd essence, held
in a shaking cup, spilt
by a spit of lead, saved
by chance alone
very real
in its silky bag of skin, its bond of bone,
so little and so limited,
there's no extenuation then.
Fate is in facts: the only hope
an unknown chance.

So I have won through. What now?
Will faith rise triumphant from the wreck
despair once more evaded in a bold
assertion of the self: self to God related
self in God attain'd, self a segment
of the eternal circle, the wheel
of Heaven, which through the dust of days
and stagnant darkness steadily revolves?

Your gentian eyes stared from the cold
impassive alp of death. You betrayed us
at the last hour of the last day
a smile your only comment
on the well-done deed. What mind
have you carried over the confines?
Your fair face was noble of its kind
some visionary purpose cut the lines
clearly on that countenance.
But you are defeated: once again
the meek inherit the kingdom of God.
No might can win against this wandering
wavering grace of humble men.

You die, in all your power and pride:
I live, in my meekness justified.

When first this fury caught us, then
I vowed devotion to the rights of men
would fight for peace once it came again
from this unwilled war pass gallantly
to wars of will and justice.
That was before I had faced death
day in day out, before hope had sunk
to a little pool of bitterness.
Now I see, either the world is mechanic force
and this the last tragic act, portending
endless hate and blind reversion
back to the tents and healthy lusts
of animal men: or we act
God's purpose in an obscure way.
Evil can only to the Reason stand
in scheme or scope beyond the human mind.
God seeks the perfect man, plann'd
to love him as a friend: our savage fate
a fire to burn our dross
to temper us to finer stock
man emerging in some inconceived span
as something more than remnant of a dream.

To that end worship God, join the voices
heard by these waking ears. God is love:
in his will the meek heart rejoices
doubting till the final grace a dove
from Heaven descends and wakes the mind
in light above the light of human kind
in light celestial
infinite and still
eternal
bright
1933

A Short Poem for Armistice Day

Gather or take fierce degree
trim the lamp set out for sea
here we are at the workmen's entrance
clock in and shed your eminence.

Notwithstanding, work it diverse ways
work it diverse days, multiplying four digestions
here we make artificial flowers
of paper tin and metal thread.

One eye one leg one arm one lung
a syncopated sick heart-beat
the record is not nearly worn
that weaves a background to our work.

I have no power therefore have patience
These flowers have no sweet scent
no lustre in the petal no increase
from fertilising flies and bees.

No seed they have no seed
their tendrils are of wire and grip
the buttonhole the lip
and never fade

And will not fade though life
and lustre go in genuine flowers
and men like flowers are cut
and wither on a stem

And will not fade a year or more
I stuck one in a candlestick
and there it clings about the socket
I have no power therefore have patience.

DAVID JONES

From *In Parenthesis*, **Part 7**

But sweet sister death has gone debauched today and
stalks on this high ground with strumpet confidence,
makes no coy veiling of her appetite but leers from you
to me with all her parts discovered.
  By one and one the line gaps, where her fancy will –
howsoever they may howl for their virginity
she holds them – who impinge less on space
sink limply to a heap
nourish a lesser category of being
like those other who fructify the land . . .

But how intolerably bright the morning is where we who
are alive and remain, walk lifted up, carried forward by
an effective word.

But red horses now – blare every trump without
economy, burn boat and sever every tie every held thing
goes west and tethering snapt, bolts unshot and brass
doors flung wide and you go forward, foot goes another
step further.

The immediate foreground sheers up, tilts toward,
like an high wall falling.
There she breaches black perpendiculars
where the counter-barrage warms to the seventh power
    where
the Three Children walk under the fair morning
and the Twin Brother

and the high grass soddens through your puttees
and dew asperges the freshly dead . . .

Mr Jenkins half inclined his head to them – he walked
just barely in advance of his platoon and immediately
to the left of Private Ball.
   He makes the conventional sign
and there is the deeply inward effort of spent men who
     would
make response for him,
and take it at the double.
He sinks on one knee
and now on the other,
his upper body tilts in rigid inclination
this way and back;
weighted lanyard runs out to full tether,
                swings like a pendulum
                  and the clock run down.
Lurched over, jerked iron saucer over tilted brow,
clampt unkindly over lip and chin
nor no ventaille to this darkening
          and masked face-lifts to grope the air
and so disconsolate;
enfeebled fingering at a paltry strap –
buckle holds,
holds him blind against the morning . . .

   His light stick-bomb winged above your thorn-bush,
and aged oak-timbers shiver and leaves shower like
thrown blossom for a conqueror.
You tug at rusted pin –
it gives unexpectedly and your fingers pressed to released
flange.
You loose the thing into the underbrush.
   Dark-faceted iron oval lobs heavily to fungus-
cushioned dank, wobbles under low leaf to lie, near
where the heel drew out just now; and tough root-fibres

boomerang to top-most green filigree and earth clods
flung disturb fresh fragile shoots that brush the sky.
    You huddle closer to your mossy bed
you make yourself scarce
you scramble forward and pretend not to see,
but ruby drops from young beech-sprigs –
are bright your hands and face.
    And the other one cries from the breaking-buckthorn.
    He calls for Elsa, for Manuela
for the parish priest of Burkersdorf in Saxe Altenburg.
    You grab his dropt stick-bomb as you go, but somehow
you don't fancy it and anyway you forget how it works.
You definitely like the coloured label on the handle,
you throw it to the tall wood-weeds . . .

they could quite easily train dark muzzles
to fiery circuit
and run with flame stabs to and fro among
stammer a level traversing
and get a woeful cross-section on
stamen-twined and bruised pistilline
steel-shorn of style and ovary
leaf and blossoming
with flora-spangled khaki pelvises
and where rustling, where limbs thrust –
        from nurturing sun hidden,
late-flowering dog-rose spray let fly like bowyer's ash,
disturbed for the movement
for the pressing forward, bodies in the bower
where adolescence walks the shrieking wood.

He watches where you lift a knee joint gingerly, to
avoid low obstacles,
with flexed articulation poked
from young leaves parted
        – and plug and splinter
shin and fibula

and twice-dye with crimson moistening
for draggled bloodwort and the madder sorrel.

   And covering every small outlet and possible sally-
way and playing old harry with any individual or
concerted effort of these to debouch or even get a dekko
of his dispositions . . .

But it's no good you cant do it with these toy spades,
you want axes, heavy iron for tough anchoring roots,
tendoned deep down.

   When someone brought up the Jerry picks it was
better, and you did manage to make some impression.
And the next one to you, where he bends to delve gets
it in the middle body. Private Ball is not instructed, and
how could you stay so fast a tide, it would be difficult
with him screaming whenever you move him ever so
little, let alone try with jack-knife to cut clear the
hampering cloth.

The First Field Dressing is futile as frantic seaman's
shift bunged to stoved bulwark, so soon the darking
flood percolates and he dies in your arms.

   And get back to that digging can't yer –
this aint a bloody Wake

            for these dead, who soon will have their dead
for burial clods heaped over.
Nor time for halsing
nor to clip green wounds
nor weeping Maries bringing anointments
neither any word spoken
nor no decent nor appropriate sowing of this seed
nor remembrance of the harvesting
of the renascent cycle
and return
nor shaving of the head nor ritual incising for these
viriles under each tree.

   No one sings: Lully lully

for the mate whose blood runs down.
Corposant his signal flare
            makes its slow parabola
where acorn hanging cross-trees tangle
and the leafy tops intersect.
And white faces lie,
(like china saucers tilted run soiling stains half dry,
when the moon shines on a scullery-rack and Mr and
Mrs Billington are asleep upstairs and so's Vi – and any
creak frightens you) or any twig moving . . .

But you seek him alive from bushment and briar –
            perhaps he's where the hornbeam spreads:
he finds you everywhere.
Where his fiery sickle garners you:
fanged-flash and darkt-fire thrring and thrrung athwart
thdrill a Wimshurst pandemonium drill with dynamo
druv staccato bark at you like Berthe Krupp's terrier
bitch and rattlesnakes for bare legs; sweat you on the
sudden like masher Bimp's back-firing No. 3 model for
Granny Bodger at 1.30 a.m. rrattle a chatter you like a
Vitus neurotic, harrow your vertebrae, bore your brain-
pan before you can say Fanny – and comfortably over
open sights:
    the gentleman must be mowed.
And to Private Ball it came as if a rigid beam of great
weight flailed about his calves, caught from behind by
ballista-baulk let fly or aft-beam slewed to clout gunnel-
walker
below below below.
    When golden vanities make about,
                    you've got no legs to stand on.
    He thought it disproportionate in its violence
considering the fragility of us.
    The warm fluid percolates between his toes and his
left boot fills, as when you tread in a puddle – he
crawled away in the opposite direction.

It's difficult with the weight of the rifle.
Leave it – under the oak.
Leave it for a salvage-bloke
let it lie bruised for a monument
dispense the authenticated fragments to the faithful . . .

   Marry it man! Marry it!
Cherish her, she's your very own.
   Coax it man coax it – it's delicately and ingeniously
made – it's an instrument of precision – it costs us
tax-payers, money – I want you men to remember that.
   Fondle it like a granny – talk to it – consider it as
you would a friend – and when you ground these arms
she's not a rooky's gas-pipe for greenhorns to tarnish.
   You've known her hot and cold.
You would choose her from among many.
You know her by her bias, and by her exact error at
300, and by the deep scar at the small, by the fair flaw
in the grain, above the lower sling-swivel –
but leave it under the oak . . .

The secret princes between the leaning trees have
diadems given them.
   Life the leveller hugs her impudent equality – she
may proceed at once to less discriminating zones.

The Queen of the Woods has cut bright boughs of
various flowering.
   These knew her influential eyes. Her awarding hands
can pluck for each their fragile prize.
   She speaks to them according to precedence. She
knows what's due to this elect society. She can choose
twelve gentle-men. She knows who is most lord between
the high trees and on the open down.
   Some she gives white berries
       some she gives brown
  Emil has a curious crown it's
      made of golden saxifrage.

Fatty wears sweet-briar,
he will reign with her for a thousand years.

For Balder she reaches high to fetch his.

Ulrich smiles for his myrtle wand.

That swine Lillywhite has daisies to his chain – you'd hardly credit it.

She plaits torques of equal splendour for Mr Jenkins and Billy Crower.

Hansel with Gronwy share dog-violets for a palm, where they lie in serious embrace beneath the twisted tripod.

Siôn gets St John's Wort – that's fair enough.

Dai Great-coat, she can't find him anywhere – she calls both high and low, she had a very special one for him.

Among this July noblesse she is mindful of December wood – when the trees of the forest beat against each other because of him.

She carries to Aneirin-in-the-nullah a rowan sprig, for the glory of Guenedota. You couldn't hear what she said to him, because she was careful for the Disciplines of the Wars.

At the gate of the wood you try a last adjustment, but slung so, it's an impediment, it's of detriment to your hopes, you had best be rid of it – the sagging webbing and all and what's left of your two fifty – but it were wise to hold on to your mask.

You're clumsy in your feebleness, you implicate your tin-hat rim with the slack sling of it.

Let it lie for the dews to rust it, or ought you to decently cover the working parts.

Its dark barrel, where you leave it under the oak, reflects the solemn star that rises urgently from Cliff Trench.

It's a beautiful doll for us
it's the Last Reputable Arm.
   But leave it – under the oak.
leave it for a Cook's tourist to the Devastated Areas and
crawl as far as you can and wait for the bearers.

Mrs Willy Hartington has learned to draw sheets and so
    has
Miss Melpomené; and on the south lawns,
men walk in red white and blue
under the cedars
and by every green tree
and beside comfortable waters.

But why dont the bastards come –
Bearers! – stret-cher bear-errs!
or do they divide the spoils at the Aid-Post.
   But how many men do you suppose could bear away
a third of us:
drag just a little further – he yet may counter-attack.

Lie still under the oak
next to the Jerry
and Sergeant Jerry Coke.
   The feet of the reserves going up tread level with your
forehead; and no word for you; they whisper one with
another; pass on inward;
these latest succours:
green Kimmerii to bear up the war.

Oeth and Annoeth's hosts they were
who in that night grew
younger men
younger striplings.

The geste says this and the man who was on the field
. . . and who wrote the book . . . the man who does not
know this has not understood anything.

HAROLD MONRO

From 'Youth in Arms'

IV *Carrion*

It is plain now what you are. Your head has dropped
Into a furrow. And the lovely curve
Of your strong leg has wasted and is propped
Against a ridge of the ploughed land's watery swerve.

You are swayed on waves of the silent ground;
You clutch and claim with passionate grasp of your fingers
The dip of earth in which your body lingers;
If you are not found,
In a little while your limbs will fall apart;
The birds will take some, but the earth will take most
    your heart.

You are fuel for a coming spring if they leave you
    here;
The crop that will rise from your bones is healthy bread.
You died – we know you – without a word of fear,
And as they loved you living I love you dead.

No girl would kiss you. But then
No girls would ever kiss the earth
In the manner they hug the lips of men:
You are not known to them in this, your second birth.

No coffin-cover now will cram
Your body in a shell of lead;
Earth will not fall on you from the spade with a slam,
But will fold and enclose you slowly, you living dead.

Hush, I hear the guns. Are you still asleep?
Surely I saw you a little heave to reply.
I can hardly think you will not turn over and creep
Along the furrows trenchward as if to die.

In the Dordogne

We stood up before day
and shaved by metal mirrors
in the faint flame of a faulty candle.

And we hurried down the wide stone stairs
with a clirr of spurr chains
on stone. And we thought
when the cocks crew
that the ghosts of a dead dawn
would rise and be off. But they stayed
under the window, crouched on the staircase,
the window now the colour of morning.

The colonel slept in the bed of Sully,
slept on: but we descended
and saw in a niche in the white wall
a Virgin and child, serene
who were stone: we saw sycamore:
three aged mages
scattering gifts of gold.
But when the wind blew, there were autumn odours
and the shadowed trees
had the dapplings of young fawns.

And each day one died or another
died: each week we sent out thousands
that returned by hundreds
wounded or gassed. And those that died
we buried close to the old wall

within a stone's throw of Perigord
under the tower of the troubadours.

And because we had courage;
because there was courage and youth
ready to be wasted; because we endured
and were prepared for all the endurance;
we thought something must come of it:
that the Virgin would raise her child and smile;
the trees gather up their gold and go;
that courage would avail something
and something we had never lost
be regained through wastage, by dying,
by burying the others under the English tower.

The colonel slept on in the bed of Sully
under the ravelling curtains: the leaves fell
and were blown away: the young men rotted
under the shadow of the tower
in a land of small clear silent streams
where the coming on of evening is
the letting down of blue and azure veils
over the clear and silent streams
delicately bordered by poplars.

Grotesque

These are the damned circles Dante trod,
Terrible in hopelessness,
But even skulls have their humour,
An eyeless and sardonic mockery:
And we,
Sitting with streaming eyes in the acrid smoke,
That murks our foul, damp billet,
Chant bitterly, with raucous voices
As a choir of frogs
In hideous irony, our patriotic songs.

Exposure

Our brains ache, in the merciless iced east winds that
   knive us . . .
Wearied we keep awake because the night is silent . . .
Low, drooping flares confuse our memory of the salient, . . .
Worried by silence, sentries whisper, curious, nervous,
         But nothing happens.

Watching, we hear the mad gusts tugging on the wire,
Like twitching agonies of men among its brambles.
Northward incessantly, the flickering gunnery rumbles,
Far off, like a dull rumour of some other war.
         What are we doing here?

The poignant misery of dawn begins to grow . . .
We only know war lasts, rain soaks, and clouds sag
   stormy.
Dawn massing in the east her melancholy army
Attacks once more in ranks on shivering ranks of gray,
         But nothing happens.

Sudden successive flights of bullets streak the silence.
Less deathly than the air that shudders black with snow
With sidelong flowing flakes that flock, pause, and renew
We watch them wandering up and down the wind's
   nonchalance,
         But nothing happens.

Pale flakes with fingering stealth come feeling for our
   faces.

We cringe in holes, back on forgotten dreams, and stare,
   snow-dazed,
Deep into grassier ditches. So we drowse, sun-dozed,
Littered with blossoms trickling where the blackbird
   fusses.
         – Is it that we are dying?

Slowly our ghosts drag home: glimpsing the sunk fires,
   glozed
With crusted dark-red jewels; crickets jingle there;
For hours the innocent mice rejoice: the house is theirs;
Shutters and doors, all closed: on us the doors are
   closed, –
         We turn back to our dying.

Since we believe not otherwise can kind fires burn;
Nor ever suns smile true on child, or field, or fruit.
For God's invincible spring our love is made afraid;
Therefore, not loath, we lie out here; therefore were
   born,
         For love of God seems dying.

To-night, this frost will fasten on this mud and us,
Shrivelling many hands, puckering foreheads crisp.
The burying-party, picks and shovels in shaking grasp,
Pause over half-known faces. All their eyes are ice,
         But nothing happens.

The Dead-Beat

He dropped, more sullenly, than wearily,
   Became a lump of stench, a clot of meat,
   And none of us could kick him to his feet.
He blinked at my revolver, blearily.

He didn't seem to know a war was on,
  Or see or smell the bloody trench at all . . .
  Perhaps he saw the crowd at Caxton Hall,
And that is why the fellow's pluck's all gone –

Not that the Kaiser frowns imperially.
  He sees his wife, how cosily she chats;
  Not his blue pal there, feeding fifty rats.
Hotels he sees, improved materially;

Where ministers smile ministerially.
  Sees Punch still grinning at the Belcher bloke;
  Bairnsfather, enlarging on his little joke,
While Belloc prophecies of last year, serially.

We sent him down at last, he seemed so bad,
  Although a strongish chap and quite unhurt.
  Next day I heard the Doc's fat laugh: 'That dirt
You sent me down last night's just died. So glad!'

Enclosed in a letter of 22 August 1917 to Owen's cousin, Leslie Gunston. Owen wrote: 'after leaving him, I wrote something in Sassoon's style'.

Dulce Et Decorum Est

Bent double, like old beggars under sacks,
Knock-kneed, coughing like hags, we cursed through
    sludge,
Till on the haunting flares we turned our backs
And towards our distant rest began to trudge.
Men marched asleep. Many had lost their boots
But limped on, blood-shod. All went lame; all blind;

Drunk with fatigue; deaf even to the hoots
Of gas shells dropping softly behind.[1]

Gas! GAS! Quick, boys! – An ecstasy of fumbling,
Fitting the clumsy helmets just in time;
But someone still was yelling out and stumbling,
And flound'ring like a man in fire or lime . . .
Dim, through the misty panes and thick green light,
As under a green sea, I saw him drowning.

In all my dreams, before my helpless sight,
He plunges at me, guttering, choking, drowning.

If in some smothering dreams you too could pace
Behind the wagon that we flung him in,
And watch the white eyes writhing in his face,
His hanging face, like a devil's sick of sin;
If you could hear, at every jolt, the blood
Come gargling from the froth-corrupted lungs,
Obscene as cancer, bitter as the cud
Of vile, incurable sores on innocent tongues, –
My friend, you would not tell with such high zest
To children ardent for some desperate glory,
The old Lie: Dulce et decorum est
Pro patria mori.

Anthem for Doomed Youth*

What passing-bells for these who die as cattle?
  – Only the monstrous anger of the guns.
   Only the stuttering rifles' rapid rattle
Can patter out their hasty orisons.

---

[1] With Edmund Blunden I read: 'Of gas-shells dropping softly be-
hind.' *The Poems of Wilfred Owen*, edited with a memoir and notes by
Edmund Blunden, Chatto & Windus, 1933.

No mockeries now for them; no prayers nor bells;
   Nor any voice of mourning save the choirs, –
The shrill, demented choirs of wailing shells;
   And bugles calling for them from sad shires.

What candles may be held to speed them all?
   Not in the hands of boys, but in their eyes
Shall shine the holy glimmers of goodbyes.
   The pallor of girls' brows shall be their pall;
Their flowers the tenderness of patient minds,
And each slow dusk a drawing-down of blinds.

Disabled

He sat in a wheeled chair, waiting for dark,
And shivered in his ghastly suit of grey,
Legless, sewn short at elbow. Through the park
Voices of boys rang saddening like a hymn,
Voices of play and pleasure after day,
Till gathering sleep had mothered them from him.

        *   *   *

About this time Town used to swing so gay
When glow-lamps budded in the light blue trees,
And girls glanced lovelier as the air grew dim,
– In the old times, before he threw away his knees.
Now he will never feel again how slim
Girls' waists are, or how warm their subtle hands.
All of them touch him like some queer disease.

        *   *   *

There was an artist silly for his face,
For it was younger than his youth, last year.
Now, he is old; his back will never brace;
He's lost his colour very far from here,
Poured it down shell-holes till the veins ran dry,
And half his lifetime lapsed in the hot race
And leap of purple spurted from his thigh.

One time he liked a bloodsmear down his leg,
After the matches, carried shoulder-high.
It was after football, when he'd drunk a peg,
He thought he'd better join. – He wonders why.
Someone had said he'd look a god in kilts,
That's why; and maybe, too, to please his Meg,
Aye, that was it, to please the giddy jilts
He asked to join. He didn't have to beg;
Smiling they wrote his lie: aged nineteen years.
Germans he scarcely thought of; all their guilt
And Austria's, did not move him. And no fears
Of Fear came yet. He thought of jewelled hilts
For daggers in plaid socks; of smart salutes;
And care of arms; and leave; and pay arrears;
Esprit de corps; and hints for young recruits.
And soon, he was drafted out with drums and cheers.

* * *

Some cheered him home, but not as crowds cheer Goal.
Only a solemn man who brought him fruits
Thanked him; and then inquired about his soul.

* * *

Now, he will spend a few sick years in institutes,
And do what things the rules consider wise,
And take whatever pity they may dole.
Tonight he noticed how the women's eyes
Passed from him to the strong men that were whole.
How cold and late it is! Why don't they come
And put him into bed? Why don't they come?

Miners

There was a whispering in my hearth,
   A sigh of the coal,
Grown wistful of a former earth
   It might recall.

I listened for a tale of leaves
    And smothered ferns;
Frond-forests; and the low, sly lives
    Before the fawns.

My fire might show steam-phantoms simmer
    From Time's old cauldron,
Before the birds made nests in summer,
    Or men had children.

But the coals were murmuring of their mine,
    And moans down there
Of boys that slept wry sleep, and men
    Writhing for air.

And I saw white bones in the cinder-shard,
    Bones without number;
For many hearts with coal are charred,
    And few remember.

I thought of some who worked dark pits
    Of war, and died
Digging the rock where Death reputes
    Peace lies indeed.

Comforted years will sit soft-chaired
    In rooms of amber;
The years will stretch their hands, well-cheered
    By our lives' ember.

The centuries will burn rich loads
    With which we groaned,
Whose warmth shall lull their dreaming lids,
    While songs are crooned.
But they will not dream of us poor lads,
    Lost in the ground.

Apologia Pro Poemate Meo

I, too, saw God through mud, –
    The mud that cracked on cheeks when wretches
      smiled.
    War brought more glory to their eyes than blood,
    And gave their laughs more glee than shakes a child.

Merry it was to laugh there –
    Where death becomes absurd and life absurder.
    For power was on us as we slashed bones bare
    Not to feel sickness or remorse of murder.

I, too, have dropped off Fear –
    Behind the barrage, dead as my platoon,
    And sailed my spirit surging light and clear
    Past the entanglement where hopes lay strewn;

And witnessed exultation –
    Faces that used to curse me, scowl for scowl,
    Shine and lift up with passion of oblation,
    Seraphic for an hour; though they were foul.

I have made fellowships –
    Untold of happy lovers in old song.
    For love is not the binding of fair lips
    With the soft silk of eyes that look and long,

By Joy, whose ribbon slips, –
    But wound with war's hard wire whose stakes are
      strong;
    Bound with the bandage of the arm that drips;
    Knit in the webbing of the rifle-thong.

I have perceived much beauty
    In the hoarse oaths that kept our courage straight;
    Heard music in the silentness of duty;
    Found peace where shell-storms spouted reddest spate.

Nevertheless, except you share
    With them in hell the sorrowful dark of hell,
    Whose world is but the trembling of a flare
    And heaven but as the highway for a shell,

You shall not hear their mirth:
    You shall not come to think them well content
    By any jest of mine. These men are worth
    Your tears. You are not worth their merriment.
November 1917

The Show

We have fallen in the dreams the ever-living
Breathe on the tarnished mirror of the world,
And then smooth out with ivory hands and sigh.
                                        W. B. YEATS

My soul looked down from a vague height, with Death,
As unremembering how I rose or why,
And saw a sad land, weak with sweats of dearth,
Gray, cratered like the moon with hollow woe,
And pitted with great pocks and scabs of plagues.

Across its beard, that horror of harsh wire,
There moved thin caterpillars, slowly uncoiled.
It seemed they pushed themselves to be as plugs
Of ditches, where they writhed and shrivelled, killed.

By them had slimy paths been trailed and scraped
Round myriad warts that might be little hills.

From gloom's last dregs these long-strung creatures
    crept,
And vanished out of dawn down hidden holes.

(And smell came up from those foul openings
As out of mouths, or deep wounds deepening.)

On dithering feet up-gathered, more and more,
Brown strings, towards strings of gray, with bristling
   spines,
All migrants from green fields, intent on mire.

Those that were gray, of more abundant spawns,
Ramped on the rest and ate them and were eaten.

I saw their bitten backs curve, loop, and straighten.
I watched those agonies curl, lift, and flatten.

Whereat, in terror what that sight might mean,
I reeled and shivered earthward like a feather.

And Death fell with me, like a deepening moan.

And He, picking a manner of worm, which half had hid
Its bruises in the earth, but crawled no further,
Showed me its feet, the feet of many men,
And the fresh-severed head of it, my head.

Insensibility

I

Happy are men who yet before they are killed
Can let their veins run cold.
Whom no compassion fleers
Or makes their feet
Sore on the alleys cobbled with their brothers.
The front line withers.
But they are troops who fade, not flowers,
For poets' tearful fooling:
Men, gaps for filling:

Losses, who might have fought
Longer; but no one bothers.

II

And some cease feeling
Even themselves or for themselves.
Dullness best solves
The tease and doubt of shelling,
And Chance's strange arithmetic
Comes simpler than the reckoning of their shilling.
They keep no check on armies' decimation.

III

Happy are these who lose imagination:
They have enough to carry with ammunition.
Their spirit drags no pack.
Their old wounds, save with cold, can not more ache.
Having seen all things red,
Their eyes are rid
Of the hurt of the colour of blood for ever.
And terror's first constriction over,
Their hearts remain small-drawn.
Their senses in some scorching cautery of battle
Now long since ironed,
Can laugh among the dying, unconcerned.

IV

Happy the soldier home, with not a notion
How somewhere, every dawn, some men attack,
And many sighs are drained.
Happy the lad whose mind was never trained:
His days are worth forgetting more than not.
He sings along the march
Which we march taciturn, because of dusk,
The long, forlorn, relentless trend
From larger day to huger night.

V

We wise, who with a thought besmirch
Blood over all our soul,
How should we see our task
But through his blunt and lashless eyes?
Alive, he is not vital overmuch;
Dying, not mortal overmuch;
Nor sad, nor proud,
Nor curious at all.
He cannot tell
Old men's placidity from his.

VI

But cursed are dullards whom no cannon stuns,
That they should be as stones.
Wretched are they, and mean
With paucity that never was simplicity.
By choice they made themselves immune
To pity and whatever moans in man
Before the last sea and the hapless stars;
Whatever mourns when many leave these shores;
Whatever shares
The eternal reciprocity of tears.

À Terre

(being the philosophy of many soldiers)

Sit on the bed. I'm blind, and three parts shell.
Be careful; can't shake hands now; never shall.
Both arms have mutinied against me, – brutes.
My fingers fidget like ten idle brats.

I tried to peg out soldierly, – no use!
One dies of war like any old disease.

This bandage feels like pennies on my eyes.
I have my medals? – Discs to make eyes close.
My glorious ribbons? – Ripped from my own back
In scarlet shreds. (That's for your poetry book.)

A short life and a merry one my buck!
We used to say we'd hate to live dead-old, –
Yet now . . . I'd willingly be puffy, bald,
And patriotic. Buffers catch from boys
At least the jokes hurled at them. I suppose
Little I'd ever teach a son, but hitting,
Shooting, war, hunting, all the arts of hurting.
Well, that's what I learnt, – that, and making money.

Your fifty years ahead seem none too many?
Tell me how long I've got? God! For one year
To help myself to nothing more than air!
One Spring! Is one too good to spare, too long?
Spring wind would work its own way to my lung,
And grow me legs as quick as lilac-shoots.

My servant's lamed, but listen how he shouts!
When I'm lugged out, he'll still be good for that.
Here in this mummy-case, you know, I've thought
How well I might have swept his floors for ever.
I'd ask no nights off when the bustle's over,
Enjoying so the dirt. Who's prejudiced
Against a grimed hand when his own's quite dust,
Less live than specks that in the sun-shafts turn,
Less warm than dust that mixes with arms' tan?
I'd love to be a sweep, now, black as Town,
Yes, or a muckman. Must I be his load?

O Life, Life, let me breathe, – a dug-out rat!
Not worse than ours the existences rats lead –
Nosing along at night down some safe rut,
They find a shell-proof home before they rot.
Dead men may envy living mites in cheese,

Or good germs even. Microbes have their joys,
And subdivide, and never come to death.
Certainly flowers have the easiest time on earth.
'I shall be one with nature, herb, and stone',
Shelley would tell me. Shelley would be stunned:
The dullest Tommy hugs that fancy now.
'Pushing up daisies' is their creed you know.
To grain, then, go my fat, to buds my sap,
For all the usefulness there is in soap.
D'you think the Boche will ever stew man-soup?
Some day, no doubt, if . . .

                     Friend, be very sure
I shall be better off with plants that share
More peaceably the meadow and the shower.
Soft rains will touch me, – as they could touch once,
And nothing but the sun shall make me ware.
Your guns may crash around me. I'll not hear;
Or, if I wince, I shall not know I wince.

Don't take my soul's poor comfort for your jest.
Soldiers may grow a soul when turned to fronds,
But here the thing's best left at home with friends.

My soul's a little grief, grappling your chest,
To climb your throat on sobs; easily chased
On other sighs and wiped by fresher winds.

Carry my crying spirit till it's weaned
To do without what blood remained these wounds.

From 'Wild with All Regrets'

Yes, there's the orderly. He'll change the sheets
When I'm lugged out. Oh, couldn't I do that?
Here in this coffin of a bed, I've thought
I'd like to kneel and sweep his floors for ever, –

And ask no nights off when the bustle's over,
For I'd enjoy the dirt. Who's prejudiced
Against a grimed hand when his own's quite dust, –
Less live than specks that in the sun-shafts turn?
Dear dust – in rooms, on roads, on faces' tan!
I'd love to be a sweep's boy, black as Town;
Yes, or a muck-man. Must I be his load?
A flea would do. If one chap wasn't bloody,
Or went stone-cold, I'd find another body.

The Send-Off

Down the close darkening lanes they sang their way
To the siding-shed,
And lined the train with faces grimly gay.

Their breasts were stuck all white with wreath and spray
As men's are, dead.

Dull porters watched them, and a casual tramp
Stood staring hard,
Sorry to miss them from the upland camp.
Then, unmoved, signals nodded, and a lamp
Winked to the guard.

So secretly, like wrongs hushed-up, they went.
They were not ours:
We never heard to which front these were sent.

Nor there if they yet mock what women meant
Who gave them flowers.

Shall they return to beatings of great bells
In wild train-loads?
A few, a few, too few for drums and yells,

May creep back, silent, to village wells,
Up half-known roads.

Mental Cases

Who are these? Why sit they here in twilight?
Wherefore rock they, purgatorial shadows,
Drooping tongues from jaws that slob their relish,
Baring teeth that leer like skulls' teeth wicked?
Stroke on stroke of pain, – but what slow panic,
Gouged these chasms round their fretted sockets?
Ever from their hair and through their hands' palms
Misery swelters. Surely we have perished
Sleeping, and walk hell; but who these hellish?

– These are men whose minds the Dead have ravished.
Memory fingers in their hair of murders,
Multitudinous murders they once witnessed.
Wading sloughs of flesh these helpless wander,
Treading blood from lungs that had loved laughter.
Always they must see these things and hear them,
Batter of guns and shatter of flying muscles,
Carnage incomparable, and human squander
Rucked too thick for these men's extrication.

Therefore still their eyeballs shrink tormented
Back into their brains, because on their sense
Sunlight seems a bloodsmear; night comes blood-black;
Dawn breaks open like a wound that bleeds afresh.
– Thus their heads wear this hilarious, hideous,
Awful falseness of set-smiling corpses.
– Thus their hands are plucking at each other;
Picking at the rope-knouts of their scourging;
Snatching after us who smote them, brother,
Pawing us who dealt them war and madness.

Futility

Move him into the sun, –
Gently its touch awoke him once,
At home, whispering of fields unsown.
Always it woke him, even in France,
Until this morning and this snow.
If anything might rouse him now
The kind old sun will know.

Think how it wakes the seeds, –
Woke, once, the clays of a cold star.
Are limbs, so dear-achievèd, are sides,
Full-nerved, – still warm, – too hard to stir?
Was it for this the clay grew tall?
– O what made fatuous sunbeams toil
To break earth's sleep at all?

Strange Meeting[1]

It seemed that out of battle I escaped
Down some profound dull tunnel, long since scooped

[1] A printed version of the manuscript of 'Strange Meeting' is provided
for the reader on account of the ambiguity in the B.M. manuscript.
What is *printed* in the main text is almost universally regarded as
Owen's final version, yet it is not clear we should so regard it. Line 39
('Foreheads of men') is always printed in the place it appears here;
but the reader will see that the pencilled (later) arrow removes it from
its received place to either the last or penultimate line. 'Let us sleep
now . . .' is also a later (pencilled) addition, subsequently inked in. If
we accept one addition, should we not also incorporate others? Such
a change in position re-inforces the idea of how loth the enemy was to
kill his 'friend', for to do so would have entailed the self-infliction of a
psychic wound ('Foreheads of men have bled'). On the other hand,
to move the line not only breaks up Owen's para-rhyme pairs but
also violates every reader's expectations of where this line should
be. How best serve him or her? Both positions are offered so that
we may each judge for ourselves.

Through granites which titanic wars had groined.

Yet also there encumbered sleepers groaned,
Too fast in thought or death to be bestirred.
Then, as I probed them, one sprang up, and stared
With piteous recognition in fixed eyes,
Lifting distressful hands, as if to bless.
And by his smile, I knew that sullen hall, –
By his dead smile I knew we stood in Hell.

With a thousand pains that vision's face was grained;
Yet no blood reached there from the upper ground,
And no guns thumped, or down the flues made moan.
'Strange friend,' I said, 'here is no cause to mourn.'
'None,' said that other, 'save the undone years,
The hopelessness. Whatever hope is yours,
Was my life also; I went hunting wild
After the wildest beauty in the world,
Which lies not calm in eyes, or braided hair;
But mocks the steady running of the hour,
And if it grieves, grieves richlier than here.
For by my glee might many men have laughed,
And of my weeping something had been left,
Which must die now. I mean the truth untold,
The pity of war, the pity war distilled.
Now men will go content with what we spoiled,
Or, discontent, boil bloody, and be spilled.
They will be swift with swiftness of the tigress.
None will break ranks, though nations trek from
    progress.
Courage was mine, and I had mystery,
Wisdom was mine, and I had mastery:
To miss the march of this retreating world
Into vain citadels that are not walled.
Then, when much blood had clogged their chariot-
    wheels,

Strange Meeting.

out of ~~the~~ battle
It seemed that ~~from my dug-out~~ I escaped

dull   ,long since
~~earth   nether~~
Down some profounder tunnel ~~older~~ scooped

, titanic   wars
~~plutonic~~
Through granites which ~~the nether flames~~ had groined.

~~Down all its length~~
~~Yet also there~~* encumbered sleepers groaned,
Too fast in thought or death to be bestirred.
Then, as I probed them, one sprang up, and stared
With piteous recognition in fixed eyes,
Lifting ~~his~~ distressful hands, as if to bless.
And by his smile, I knew we stood in Hell.
~~And~~ By his ~~dead~~ smile I knew that sullen hall. –
~~Yet slumber droned all down that sullen hall.~~

pains
wrongs   vision's
With a thousand ~~fears that creature's~~ face was grained;

there
reached ~~him~~
Yet no blood ~~sumped here~~ from the upper ground,

guns
And no ~~shell~~ thumped, or down the flues made moan.
~~But all was sleep. And no voice called for men.~~

'Strange
'~~My~~ friend,' I said, 'Here is no cause to mourn.'
'None,' said that other, 'Save the undone years,

~~unachieved.~~
~~unsure~~
The ~~hopelessness.~~ Whatever hope is yours,

~~for~~   hunting
;I went   I hunted
Was my life also, ~~comrade. I ran~~ wild
After the wildest beauty in the world,
Which lies not calm in eyes, or braided hair;

But mocks the steady running of the hour.
And if it grieves, grieves richlier than here.
For by my glee might many men have laughed,
And of my weeping something had been left,
Which must die now. I mean the truth untold,

        pity
The pity of war, the ~~one thing~~ war distilled.
Now men will go content with what we spoiled,
Or, discontent, boil bloody, and be spilled.
They will be swift with swiftness of the tigress.
None will break ranks, though nations trek from progress.
Courage was mine, and I had mystery,
Wisdom was mine, and I had mastery:
To miss the march of this retreating world
Into vain citadels that are not walled.
Then, when much blood had clogged their chariot-wheels
I would go up and wash them from sweet wells,

     with truths
       ~~thoughts that~~ lie
Even ~~the wells I sank~~ too deep for taint.
I would have poured my spirit without stint

      through wounds; not on
         to   ~~mire~~
But not ~~by my blood in~~ the ~~cess~~ of war.
Foreheads of men have bled where no wounds were.

     enemy
  am the ~~German whom~~ you killed, my
I ~~was a German conscript, and your~~ friend.
I knew you in this dark: for so you frowned
Yesterday through me as you jabbed and killed.
~~I parried; but my hands were loath and~~ cold.
    Let us ~~sleep now~~ . . . .

*'Yet also there' is restored in every editing

I would go up and wash them from sweet wells,
Even with truths that lie too deep for taint.
I would have poured my spirit without stint
But not through wounds; not on the cess of war.
Foreheads of men have bled where no wounds were.
I am the enemy you killed, my friend.
I knew you in this dark: for so you frowned
Yesterday through me as you jabbed and killed.
I parried; but my hands were loath and cold.
Let us sleep now . . .'

The Sentry

We'd found an old Boche dug-out, and he knew,
And gave us hell, for shell on frantic shell
Hammered on top, but never quite burst through.
Rain, guttering down in waterfalls of slime
Kept slush waist-high, and rising hour by hour,
And choked the steps too thick with clay to climb.
What murk of air remained stank old, and sour
With fumes of whizzbangs, and the smell of men
Who'd lived there years, and left their curse in the den,
If not their corpses . . .
                                    There we herded from the blast
Of whizzbangs, but one found our door at last,
Buffeting eyes and breath, snuffing the candles,
And thud! flump! thud! down the steep steps came
    thumping
And sploshing in the flood, deluging muck –
The sentry's body; then his rifle, handles
Of old Boche bombs, and mud in ruck on ruck.
We dredged him up, for killed, until he whined
'O sir, my eyes – I'm blind, – I'm blind, I'm blind!'
Coaxing, I held a flame against his lids
And said if he could see the least blurred light

He was not blind; in time he'd get all right.
'I can't,' he sobbed. Eyeballs, huge-bulged like squids',
Watch my dreams still; but I forgot him there
In posting Next for duty, and sending a scout
To beg a stretcher somewhere, and flound'ring about
To other posts under the shrieking air.

* * *

Those other wretches, how they bled and spewed,
And one who would have drowned himself for good, –
I try not to remember these things now.
Let dread hark back for one word only: how
Half-listening to that sentry's moans and jumps,
And the wild chattering of his broken teeth,
Renewed most horribly whenever crumps
Pummelled the roof and slogged the air beneath, –
Through the dense din, I say, we heard him shout
'I see your lights!' But ours had long died out.

Smile, Smile, Smile

Head to limp head, the sunk-eyed wounded scanned
Yesterday's *Mail*; the casualties (typed small)
And (large) Vast Booty from our Latest Haul.
Also, they read of Cheap Homes, not yet planned,
For, said the paper, When this war is done
The men's first instincts will be making homes.
Meanwhile their foremost need is aerodromes,
It being certain war has but begun.
Peace would do wrong to our undying dead, –
The sons we offered might regret they died
If we got nothing lasting in their stead.
We must be solidly indemnified.
Though all be worthy Victory which all bought,
We rulers sitting in this ancient spot

Would wrong our very selves if we forgot
The greatest glory will be theirs who fought,
Who kept this nation in integrity.
Nation? – The half-limbed readers did not chafe
But smiled at one another curiously
Like secret men who know their secret safe.
(This is the thing they know and never speak,
That England one by one had fled to France,
Not many elsewhere now, save under France.)
Pictures of these broad smiles appear each week,
And people in whose voice real feeling rings
Say: How they smile! They're happy now, poor things.
23 September 1918

Spring Offensive

Halted against the shade of a last hill,
They fed, and lying easy, were at ease
And finding comfortable chests and knees
Carelessly slept. But many there stood still
To face the stark blank sky beyond the ridge
Knowing their feet had come to the end of the world.

Marvelling they stood, and watched the long grass
    swirled
By the May breeze, murmurous with wasp and midge,
For though the summer oozed into their veins
Like an injected drug for their bodies' pains,
Sharp on their souls hung the imminent line of grass,
Fearfully flashed the sky's mysterious glass.

Hour after hour they ponder the warm field, –
And the far valley behind, where the buttercup
Had blessed with gold their slow boots coming up,
Where even the little brambles would not yield

But clutched and clung to them like sorrowing hands.
[All their strange day]¹ they breathe like trees unstirred,

Till like a cold gust thrills the little word
At which each body and its soul begird
And tighten them for battle. No alarms
Of bugles, no high flags, no clamorous haste, –
Only a lift and flare of eyes that faced
The sun, like a friend with whom their love is done.
O larger shone that smile against the sun, –
Mightier than his whose bounty these have spurned.

So, soon, they topped the hill, and raced together
Over an open stretch of herb and heather
Exposed. And instantly the whole sky burned
With fury against them; earth set sudden cups
In thousands for their blood; and the green slope
Chasmed and steepened sheer to infinite space.

＊   ＊   ＊

Of them who running on that last high place
Breasted even the rapture of bullets, or went up²

---

¹ This half-line within square brackets is deleted in the B.M. manuscript. It's restored here (in brackets) firstly because no other version replaces these deletions, and then because Owen does not suggest that he wishes the remaining part of the line to conclude the syntax, which, as other editors have printed it, does give this suggestion.

² C. Day Lewis followed Edmund Blunden's reading of this line, though it is cancelled in the B.M. MS; i.e.

Leapt to swift unseen bullets, or went up

He states in a footnote: 'I am indebted to Dr Welland for the following note on this line –

"My impression is that Owen changed it as follows:
(a) *unseen* was cancelled and *surf of* substituted above
(b) he then cancelled *Leapt to the unseen* and substituted above *Breasted the shrieking*
(c) next he cancelled *the shrieking*, put in another *the* before it and *even rapture of bullets* after it, and then cancelled *Breasted*

On the hot blast and fury of hell's upsurge,
Or plunged and fell away past this world's verge,
Some say God caught them even before they fell.

But what say such as from existence' brink
Ventured but drave too swift to sink,
The few who rushed in the body to enter hell,
And there outfiending all its fiends and flames
With superhuman inhumanities,
Long-famous glories, immemorial shames –
And crawling slowly back, have by degrees
Regained cool and peaceful air in wonder –
Why speak not they of comrades that went under?

The best alternative to E.B. I can suggest is
    Breasted the surf of bullets, or went up"'

I am indebted to Day Lewis's citing of Welland's note. He has
provided a more than helpful reading of a difficult part of the MS,
but I can only add that I do not agree with his concluding product.
There is certainly room for an alternative reading which is, however,
indebted to Welland's note.

D. H. LAWRENCE

Song of a Man Who Has Come Through

Not I, not I, but the wind that blows through me!
A fine wind is blowing the new direction of Time.
If only I let it bear me, carry me, if only it carry me!
If only I am sensitive, subtle, oh, delicate, a winged gift!
If only, most lovely of all, I yield myself and am borrowed
By the fine, fine wind that takes its course through the
    chaos of the world
Like a fine, an exquisite chisel, a wedge-blade inserted;
If only I am keen and hard like the sheer tip of a wedge
Driven by invisible blows,
The rock will split, we shall come at the wonder, we
    shall find the Hesperides.
Oh, for the wonder that bubbles into my soul,
I would be a good fountain, a good well-head,
Would blur no whisper, spoil no expression.
What is the knocking?
What is the knocking at the door in the night?
It is somebody wants to do us harm.
No, no, it is the three strange angels.
Admit them, admit them.

In the 1928 edition of his *Collected Poems*, Lawrence wrote:
'So one would like to ask the reader of *Look! We Have Come
Through!* to fill in the background of the poems, as far as
possible, with the place, the time, the circumstance. What was
uttered in the cruel spring of 1917 should not be dislocated and
heard as if sounding out of the void.'

On Receiving News of the War

Snow is a strange white word.
No ice or frost
Has asked of bud or bird
For Winter's cost.

Yet ice and frost and snow
From earth to sky
This Summer land doth know.
No man knows why.

In all men's hearts it is.
Some spirit old
Hath turned with malign kiss
Our lives to mould.

Red fangs have torn His face.
God's blood is shed.
He mourns from His lone place
His children dead.

O! ancient crimson curse!
Corrode, consume.
Give back this universe
Its pristine bloom.

Cape Town, 1914

From *Moses*

MOSES: Fine! Fine!
See in my brain
What madmen have rushed through,
And like a tornado
Torn up the tight roots
Of some dead universe.
The old clay is broken
For a power to soak in and knit
It all into tougher tissues
To hold life,
Pricking my nerves till the brain might crack
It boils to my finger-tips,
Till my hands ache to grip
The hammer – the lone hammer
That breaks lives into a road
Through which my genius drives.
Pharaoh well peruked and oiled,
And your admirable pyramids,
And your interminable procession
Of crowded kings,
You are my little fishing rods
Wherewith I catch the fish
To suit my hungry belly.

I am rough now, and new, and will have no tailor.
Startlingly,
As a mountain-side
Wakes aware of its other side,
When from a cave a leopard comes,
On its heels the same red sand,
Springing with acquainted air,
Sprang an intelligence
Coloured as a whim of mine,
Showed to my dull outer eyes

The living eyes underneath.
Did I not shrivel up and take the place of air,
Secret as those eyes were,
And those strong eyes call up a giant frame?
And I am that now . . .

Egypt was in the way; I'll strike it out
With my ways curious and unusual.
I have a trouble in my mind for largeness,
Rough-hearted, shaggy, which your grave ardours lack.
Here is the quarry quiet for me to hew,
Here are the springs, primeval elements,
The roots' hid secrecy, old source of race,
Unreasoned reason of the savage instinct.
I'd shape one impulse through the contraries
Of vain ambitious men, selfish and callous,
And frail life-drifters, reticent, delicate.
Litheness thread bulk; a nation's harmony.
These are not lame, nor bent awry, but placeless
With the rust and stagnant. All that's low I'll charm;
Barbaric love sweeten to tenderness.
Cunning run into wisdom, craft turn to skill.
Their meanness threaded right and sensibly
Change to a prudence, envied and not sneered.
Their hugeness be a driving wedge to a thing,
Ineffable and useable, as near
Solidity as human life can be.
So grandly fashion these rude elements
Into some newer nature, a consciousness
Like naked light seizing the all-eyed soul,
Oppressing with its gorgeous tyranny
Until they take it thus – or die.

[*While speaking, he places his hand on the unsuspecting
Egyptian's head and gently pulls his hair back (caressingly),
until his chin is above his forehead, and holds him so till he is*

suffocated. In the darkness ahead is seen the glimmer of
javelins and spears. It is Prince Imra's cohorts come to arrest
MOSES]

Marching

(As Seen from the Left File)

My eyes catch ruddy necks
Sturdily pressed back –
All a red brick moving glint.
Like flaming pendulums, hands
Swing across the khaki –
Mustard-coloured khaki –
To the automatic feet.

We husband the ancient glory
In these bared necks and hands.
Not broke is the forge of Mars;
But a subtler brain beats iron
To shoe the hoofs of death
(Who paws dynamic air now).
Blind fingers loose an iron cloud
To rain immortal darkness
On strong eyes.

August 1914

What in our lives is burnt
In the fire of this?
The heart's dear granary?
The much we shall miss?

Three lives hath one life –
Iron, honey, gold.
The gold, the honey gone –
Left is the hard and cold.

Iron are our lives
Molten right through our youth.
A burnt space through ripe fields
A fair mouth's broken tooth.

Break of Day in the Trenches

The darkness crumbles away –
It is the same old druid Time as ever.
Only a live thing leaps my hand –
A queer sardonic rat –
As I pull the parapet's poppy
To stick behind my ear.
Droll rat, they would shoot you if they knew
Your cosmopolitan sympathies.
Now you have touched this English hand
You will do the same to a German –
Soon, no doubt, if it be your pleasure
To cross the sleeping green between.
It seems you inwardly grin as you pass
Strong eyes, fine limbs, haughty athletes
Less chanced than you for life,
Bonds to the whims of murder,
Sprawled in the bowels of the earth,
The torn fields of France.
What do you see in our eyes
At the shrieking iron and flame
Hurled through still heavens?
What quaver – what heart aghast?

Poppies whose roots are in man's veins
Drop, and are ever dropping;
But mine in my ear is safe,
Just a little white with the dust.

'A worm fed on the heart of Corinth'

A worm fed on the heart of Corinth,
Babylon and Rome:
Not Paris raped tall Helen,
But this incestuous worm,
Who lured her vivid beauty
To his amorphous sleep.
England! famous as Helen
Is thy betrothal sung
To him the shadowless,
More amorous than Solomon.

Louse Hunting

Nudes – stark and glistening,
Yelling in lurid glee. Grinning faces
And raging limbs
Whirl over the floor one fire.
For a shirt verminously busy
Yon soldier tore from his throat, with oaths
Godhead might shrink at, but not the lice.
And soon the shirt was aflare
Over the candle he'd lit while we lay.

Then we all sprang up and stript
To hunt the verminous brood.

Soon like a demons' pantomime
The place was raging.
See the silhouettes agape,
See the gibbering shadows
Mixed with the battled arms on the wall.
See gargantuan hooked fingers
Pluck in supreme flesh
To smutch supreme littleness.
See the merry limbs in hot Highland fling
Because some wizard vermin
Charmed from the quiet this revel
When our ears were half lulled
By the dark music
Blown from Sleep's trumpet.

Returning, We Hear the Larks

Sombre the night is.
And though we have our lives, we know
What sinister threat lurks there.

Dragging these anguished limbs, we only know
This poison-blasted track opens on our camp –
On a little safe sleep.

But hark! joy – joy – strange joy.
Lo! heights of night ringing with unseen larks.
Music showering on our upturned list'ning faces.

Death could drop from the dark
As easily as song –
But song only dropped,
Like a blind man's dreams on the sand
By dangerous tides,
Like a girl's dark hair for she dreams no ruin lies there,
Or her kisses where a serpent hides.

Dead Man's Dump

The plunging limbers over the shattered track
Racketed with their rusty freight,
Stuck out like many crowns of thorns,
And the rusty stakes like sceptres old
To stay the flood of brutish men
Upon our brothers dear.

The wheels lurched over sprawled dead
But pained them not, though their bones crunched,
Their shut mouths made no moan.
They lie there huddled, friend and foeman,
Man born of man, and born of woman,
And shells go crying over them
From night till night and now.

Earth has waited for them,
All the time of their growth
Fretting for their decay:
Now she has them at last!
In the strength of their strength
Suspended – stopped and held.

What fierce imaginings their dark souls lit?
Earth! have they gone into you!
Somewhere they must have gone,
And flung on your hard back
Is their soul's sack
Emptied of God-ancestralled essences.
Who hurled them out? Who hurled?

None saw their spirits' shadow shake the grass,
Or stood aside for the half used life to pass
Out of those doomed nostrils and the doomed mouth,
When the swift iron burning bee
Drained the wild honey of their youth.

What of us who, flung on the shrieking pyre,
Walk, our usual thoughts untouched,
Our lucky limbs as on ichor fed,
Immortal seeming ever?
Perhaps when the flames beat loud on us,
A fear may choke in our veins
And the startled blood may stop.

The air is loud with death,
The dark air spurts with fire,
The explosions ceaseless are.
Timelessly now, some minutes past,
These dead strode time with vigorous life,
Till the shrapnel called 'An end!'
But not to all. In bleeding pangs
Some borne on stretchers dreamed of home,
Dear things, war-blotted from their hearts.

Maniac Earth! howling and flying, your bowel
Seared by the jagged fire, the iron love,
The impetuous storm of savage love.
Dark Earth! dark Heavens! swinging in chemic smoke,
What dead are born when you kiss each soundless soul
With lightning and thunder from your mined heart,
Which man's self dug, and his blind fingers loosed?

A man's brains splattered on
A stretcher-bearer's face;
His shook shoulders slipped their load,
But when they bent to look again
The drowning soul was sunk too deep
For human tenderness.

They left this dead with the older dead,
Stretched at the cross roads.

Burnt black by strange decay
Their sinister faces lie,

The lid over each eye,
The grass and coloured clay
More motion have than they,
Joined to the great sunk silences.

Here is one not long dead;
His dark hearing caught our far wheels,
And the choked soul stretched weak hands
To reach the living word the far wheels said,
The blood-dazed intelligence beating for light,
Crying through the suspense of the far torturing wheels
Swift for the end to break
Or the wheels to break,
Cried as the tide of the world broke over his sight.

Will they come? Will they ever come?
Even as the mixed hoofs of the mules,
The quivering-bellied mules,
And the rushing wheels all mixed
With his tortured upturned sight.
So we crashed round the bend,
We heard his weak scream,
We heard his very last sound,
And our wheels grazed his dead face.

Daughters of War

Space beats the ruddy freedom of their limbs –
Their naked dances with man's spirit naked
By the root side of the tree of life
(The under side of things
And shut from earth's profoundest eyes).

I saw in prophetic gleams
These mighty daughters in their dances
Beckon each soul aghast from its crimson corpse
To mix in their glittering dances.

I heard the mighty daughters' giant sighs
In sleepless passion for the sons of valour,
And envy of the days of flesh
Barring their love with mortal boughs across –
The mortal boughs, the mortal tree of life.
The old bark burnt with iron wars
They blow to a live flame
To char the young green days
And reach the occult soul; they have no softer lure –
No softer lure than the savage ways of death.
We were satisfied of our lords the moon and the sun
To take our wage of sleep and bread and warmth –
These maidens came – these strong everliving Amazons,
And in an easy might their wrists
Of night's sway and noon's sway the sceptres brake,
Clouding the wild – the soft lustres of our eyes.

Clouding the wild lustres, the clinging tender lights;
Driving the darkness into the flame of day
With the Amazonian wind of them
Over our corroding faces
That must be broken – broken for evermore
So the soul can leap out
Into their huge embraces.
Though there are human faces
Best sculptures of Deity,
And sinews lusted after
By the Archangels tall,
Even these must leap to the love-heat of these maidens
From the flame of terrene days,
Leaving grey ashes to the wind – to the wind.

One (whose great lifted face,
Where wisdom's strength and beauty's strength
And the thewed strength of large beasts
Moved and merged, gloomed and lit)

Was speaking, surely, as the earth-men's earth fell away;
Whose new hearing drank the sound
Where pictures lutes and mountains mixed
With the loosed spirit of a thought.
Essenced to language, thus –

'My sisters force their males
From the doomed earth, from the doomed glee
And hankering of hearts.
Frail hands gleam up through the human quagmire
    and lips of ash
Seem to wail, as in sad faded paintings
Far sunken and strange.
My sisters have their males
Clean of the dust of old days
That clings about those white hands
And yearns in those voices sad.
But these shall not see them,
Or think of them in any days or years;
They are my sisters' lovers in other days and years.'

From *The Amulet*

LILITH:

      The slime clung
And licked and clawed and chewed the clogged dragging
    wheels
Till they sunk right to the axle. Saul sodden and vexed
Like fury smote the mules' mouths, pulling but sweat
From his drowned hair and theirs, while the thunder
    knocked
And all the air yawned water, falling water,
And the light cart was water, like a wrecked raft,
And all seemed like a forest under the ocean.
Sudden the lightning flashed upon a figure

Moving as a man moves in the slipping mud
But singing not as a man sings, through the storm,
Which could not drown his sounds. Saul bawled 'Hi! Hi!'
And the man loomed, naked vast, and gripped the wheels.
Saul fiercely dug from under. He tugged the wheels,
The mules foamed, straining, straining,
Sudden they went . . .

You have seen men and women,
Soaked yourself in powers and old glories,
In broken days and tears and glees,
And touched cold hands –
Hands shut in pitiless trances where the feast is high.
I think there is more sorrow in the world
Than man can bear.
NUBIAN: None can exceed their limit, lady:
You either bear or break.
LILITH: Can one choose to break? To bear,
To wearily bear, is misery.
Beauty is this corroding malady.
NUBIAN: Beauty is a great paradox –
Music's secret soul creeping about the senses
To wrestle with man's coarser nature.
It is hard when beauty loses.

The Tower of Skulls

MOURNERS

These layers of piled-up skulls,
These layers of gleaming horror – stark horror!
Ah me! Through my thin hands they touch my eyes.

Everywhere, everywhere is a pregnant birth,
And here in death's land is a pregnant birth.
Your own crying is less mortal
Than the amazing soul in your body.

Your own crying yon parrot takes up
And from your empty skull cries it afterwards.

Thou whose dark activities unenchanted
Days from gyrating days, suspending them
To thrust them far from sight, from the gyrating days
Which have gone widening on and left us here,
Cast derelicts lost for ever.

When aged flesh looks down on tender brood;
For he knows between his thin ribs' walls
The giant universe, the interminable
Panorama – synods, myths and creeds,
He knows his dust is fire and seed.

From *The Unicorn*

SAUL: Sick . . . Sick . . . I will lie down and die. How
    can I die?
Kind lightning, sweetest lightning, cleave me through
Lift up these shreds of being and mix me with
This wind, this darkness.
I'll strive once more. See how the wheels are sunk
Right to the axle . . . Ah impotent puny me . . .
Vain. Futile.
Hi hi hi hi, is there no man about?
Who would be wandering in a storm like this? –
Hark . . . was that a human voice?
Sh . . . when that crash ceases.
Like laughter . . . like laughter,
Sure that was laughter . . . just the laughter of ours.
Hi hi hi hi hi hi . . .
My voice fears me.
God cover my eyes.

LILITH: The roots of a torn universe are wrenched,
See the bent trees like nests of derelicts in ocean

That beats upon this ark.
TEL: Unearthly accents float amid the howling storm.
Her mouth moves . . . is it thence . . .
Secret Mother of my orphan spirit
Who art thou?
LILITH: I think he speaks, this howling storm sheets
  out all so.
I'll play and ease my heavy heart.
TEL: Was that the lightning?
Those fragile gleaming wrists untangle me,
Those looks tread out my soul.
Somewhere I know those looks, I lost it somewhere.

[LILITH *draws nearer and sings softly*]

LILITH: Beauty is music's secret soul,
Creeping about man's senses.
He cannot hold it or know it ever,
But yearns and yearns to hold it once.
Ah! when he yearns not shall he not wither?
For music then will have no place
In the world's ear, but mix in windless darkness . . .

TEL: Hear me, hear me.
Do I speak, or think I speak,
I am so faint . . . Wait,
Let my dazed blood resolve itself to words.
Where have I strayed . . . incomprehensible . . .
Yet here . . . somewhere
An instant flashes a large face of dusk
Like heights of night ringing with unseen larks
Or blindness dim with dreams.
I hear a low voice . . . a crooning . . .
Some whisperings, shadows vast,
A crying through the forest, wailing.

Behind impassable places
Whose air was never warmed by a woman's lips
Bestial man shapes ride dark impulses
Through roots in the bleak blood, then hide
In shuddering light from their self loathing.
They fade in arid light –
Beings unnatured by their craving, for they know
Obliteration's spectre. They are few.
They wail their souls for continuity,
And bow their heads and knock their breasts before
The many mummies whose wail in dust is more
Than these who cry, their brothers who loiter yet.
Great beasts' and small beasts' eyes have place
As eyes of women to their hopeless eyes
That hunt in bleakness for the dread might,
The incarnate female soul of generation.
The daughters of any clime are not imagined
Even of their occult ears, senses profound,
For their corporeal ears and baby senses
Were borne for gentle voices and gentle forms
By men misused flying from misuse
Who gave them suck even from their narrow breasts
Only for this, that they should wither
That they should be as an uttered sound in the wind.

[*He sees* SAUL's *smouldering eyes in the doorway. It rouses him*]

By now my men have raided the city,
I heard a far shrieking.
LILITH: This is most piteous, most fearful,
I fear him, his hungry eyes
Burn into me, like those balls of fire.
TEL: There is a tower of skulls,
Where birds make nests
And staring beasts stand by with many flocks
And man looks on with hopeless eyes . . .

LILITH: O horrible, I hear Saul rattle those chains in the
   cellar.
TEL: What clanking chains?
When a man's brains crack with longing
We chain him to some slender beast to breed.
LILITH: Tell me, tell me, who took my cousin Dora,
Oh God those balls of fire . . .
Are you men . . . ? tell me.
TEL: Marvellous creature.
Night tender beast.
Has the storm passed into me,
What ecstasy, what lightning
Has touched the lightning in my blood.
Voluptuous
Crude vast terrible hunger overpowers . . .
A gap . . . a yawning . . .
My blood knocks . . . inarticulate to make you understand,
To shut you in itself
Uncontrollable. [*He stretches his arms out*]
Small dazzling face I shut you in my soul –

[*She shrieks.* SAUL *appears, looking about dazed, holding an
iron chain; while the door is burst open and* ENOCH *bursts in.
He springs on* TEL]

ENOCH: Where is my Dora, where?
Pity, rider of the Unicorn.
TEL: Yonder.
[*Through the casement they see riding under the rainbow a
black naked host on various animals, the Unicorn leading. A
woman is clasped on every one, some are frantic, others white
or unconscious, some nestle laughing.* ENOCH *with madness in
his eyes leaps through the casement and disappears with a
splash in the well.* SAUL *leaps after him shouting 'The
Unicorn'.*
TEL *places the unconscious* LILITH *on the Unicorn and they
all ride away*]

Soldier: Twentieth Century

I love you, great new Titan!
Am I not you?
Napoleon and Caesar
Out of you grew.

Out of unthinkable torture,
Eyes kissed by death, –
Won back to the world again,
Lost and won in a breath,

Cruel men are made immortal,
Out of your pain born.
They have stolen the sun's power
With their feet on your shoulders worn.

Let them shrink from your girth,
That has outgrown the pallid days,
When you slept like Circe's swine,
Or a word in the brain's ways.

Girl to Soldier on Leave

I love you – Titan lover,
My own storm-days' Titan.
Greater than the son of Zeus,
I know whom I would choose.

Titan – my splendid rebel –
The old Prometheus
Wanes like a ghost before your power –
His pangs were joys to yours.

Pallid days arid and wan
Tied your soul fast.

Babel-cities' smoky tops
Pressed upon your growth

Weary gyves. What were you
But a word in the brain's ways,
Or the sleep of Circe's swine?
One gyve holds you yet.

It held you hiddenly on the Somme
Tied from my heart at home.
O must it loosen now? I wish
You were bound with the old old gyves.

Love! you love me – your eyes
Have looked through death at mine.
You have tempted a grave too much.
I let you – I repine.

The Burning of the Temple

Fierce wrath of Solomon
Where sleepest thou? O see
The fabric which thou won
Earth and ocean to give thee –
O look at the red skies.

Or hath the sun plunged down?
What is this molten gold –
These thundering fires blown
Through heaven – where the smoke rolled?
Again the great king dies.

His dreams go out in smoke,
His days he let not pass
And sculptured here are broke,
Are charred as the burnt grass,
Gone as his mouth's last sighs.

The Destruction of Jerusalem by the Babylonian Hordes

They left their Babylon bare
Of all its tall men,
Of all its proud horses;
They made for Lebanon.

And shadowy sowers went
Before their spears to sow
The fruit whose taste is ash
For Judah's soul to know.

They who bowed to the Bull god
Whose wings roofed Babylon,
In endless hosts darkened
The bright-heavened Lebanon.

They washed their grime in pools
Where laughing girls forgot
The wiles they used for Solomon.
Sweet laughter! remembered not.

Sweet laughter charred in the flame
That clutched the cloud and earth
While Solomon's towers crashed between,
The gird of Babylon's mirth.

GEORG HEYM

War

He is risen now that was so long asleep,
Risen out of vaulted places dark and deep.
In the growing dusk the faceless demon stands,
And the moon he crushes in his strong black hands.

In the nightfall noises of great cities fall
Frost and shadow of an unfamiliar pall.
And the maelstrom of the markets turns to ice.
Silence grows. They look around. And no one knows.

Something touching them in side-streets makes them
    quail.
Questions. There's no answer. Someone's face turns pale.
Far away a peal of church-bells trembles, thin,
Causes beards to tremble round their pointed chins.

On the mountains he's begun his battle-dance,
Calling: Warriors, up and at them, now's your chance!
There's a rattling when he shakes his brute black head
Round which crudely hang the skulls of countless dead.

Like a tower he tramples out the dying light.
Rivers are brim-full of blood by fall of night.
Legion are the bodies laid out in the reeds,
Covered white with the strong birds of death.

Ever on he drives the fire and nightward-bound,
To the screams that come from wild mouths, a red hound.
Out of darkness springs the black domain of Nights,
Edges weirdly lit up by volcanic lights.

Pointed caps unnumbered, flickering, extend
Over the satanic plains from end to end.
And he casts allfleeing things down on the roads
Into fiery forests where the swift flame roars.

Forests fall to the consuming flames in sheaves,
Yellow bats whose jagged fangs claw at the leaves.
Like a charcoal burner in the trees he turns
His great poker, making them more fiercely burn.

A great city quietly sank in yellow smoke,
Hurled itself down into that abysmal womb.
But gigantic over glowing ruins stands
He who thrice at angry heavens shakes his brand.

Over storm-torn clouds' reflected livid glow
At cold wastelands of dead darkness down below.
That his hellfire may consume this night of horror
He pours pitch and brimstone down on their Gomorrha.

1911

Translated from the German by Patrick Bridgwater.

'Why do you visit me, white moths, so often?'

Why do you visit me, white moths, so often?
You dead souls, why should you often flutter
Down to my hand, so that a little
Ash from your wings is often left there?

You who dwell among urns, there, where dreams rest,
Bowed among eternal shades, in the twilit place,
Like bats in sepulchres,
Swirling out by night with much sound.

Often in sleep I hear the barking of vampires,
Like laughter from the dull moon's honeycombs,

And see deep down in empty caverns
The tapers of the homeless shades.

What is life? A brief torchlight,
Grimaces grinning from black gloom around it,
And some approach and stretch
Their thin hands toward the flame.

What is life? A small ship in the gulfs
Of forgotten seas. Pallor of frozen skies.
Or the way lost moonlight on bare fields
Wanders in the night and vanishes.

Alas for him who ever saw a man die,
When in cool autumn's quiet, invisible,
Death walked to the sick man's damp bed
And told him he must go, when the throat

Blew with a rattle the last air out
Like the frost and whistling of a rusty organ.
Alas for him who has seen death! Evermore
He wears the white flower of leaden horror.

Who opens the countries to us after death?
And who the gateway of the monstrous rune?
What do the dying see, that makes them turn
Their eyes' blind whiteness round so terribly?
1912

Translated from the German by Christopher Middleton.

Dejection

Mighty you are, dark mouth
Within, configuration formed
Of autumn clouds,
Of golden evening stillness;
A greenishly glimmering mountain brook
In the shadow precinct
Of broken pines:
A village
That in brown images piously suffers decay.

There the black horses leap
On a hazy pasture.
You soldiers!
From the hill where dying the sun rolls
Laughing blood roars down –
Under oaks,
Speechless. O the army's
Grim dejection; a bright helmet
Clattering slid from a crimson brow.

Autumn night so coolly comes.
Lights up with stars
Above the broken bones of men
The quiet maiden monk.

June 1914

In the East

Like the wild organs of the winter storm
Is the people's gloomy rage,
The purple billow of battle
Of stars leaf-stripped.
With broken brows, silvery arms
The night beckons to dying soldiers.
In the autumnal ash-tree's shade
The ghosts of the killed are sighing.

Thorny wilderness surrounds the town.
From steps that bleed the moon
Drives off dumbfounded women.
Wild wolves have burst through the gate.

Lament

Sleep and death, the dusky eagles
Around this head swoop all night long:
Eternity's icy wave
Would swallow the golden image
Of man; against horrible reefs
His purple body is shattered.
And the dark voice laments
Over the sea.
Sister of stormy sadness,
Look a timid dinghy goes down
Under stars,
The silent face of the night.

Grodek

At nightfall the autumn woods cry out
With deadly weapons, and the golden plains
The deep blue lakes, above which more darkly
Rolls the sun; the night embraces
Dying warriors, the wild lament
Of their broken mouths.
But quietly there in the pastureland
Red clouds in which an angry god resides,
The shed blood gathers, lunar coolness.
All the roads lead to blackest carrion.
Under golden twigs of the night and stars
The sister's shade now sways through the silent copse
To greet the ghosts of the heroes, the bleeding heads;
And softly the dark flutes of autumn sound in the reeds.
O prouder grief! You brazen altars,
Today a great pain feeds the hot flame of the spirit,
The grandsons yet unborn.
1914

All poems by Georg Trakl translated from the German by
Michael Hamburger.

ALFRED LICHTENSTEIN

Leaving for the Front

Before I die I must just find this rhyme.
Be quiet, my friends, and do not waste my time.

We're marching off in company with death.
I only wish my girl would hold her breath.

There's nothing wrong with me. I'm glad to leave.
Now mother's crying too. There's no reprieve.

And now look how the sun's begun to set.
A nice mass-grave is all that I shall get.

Once more the good old sunset's glowing red.
In thirteen days I'll probably be dead.

7 August 1914:
seven weeks later Lichtenstein was dead

Translated from the German by Patrick Bridgwater.

WILHELM KLEMM

Clearing-Station

Straw rustling everywhere.
The candle-stumps stand there staring solemnly.
Across the nocturnal vault of the church
Moans go drifting and choking words.

There's a stench of blood, pus, shit and sweat.
Bandages ooze away underneath torn uniforms.
Clammy trembling hands and wasted faces.
Bodies stay propped up as their dying heads slump
    down.

In the distance the battle thunders grimly on,
Day and night, groaning and grumbling non-stop,
And to the dying men patiently waiting for their graves
It sounds for all the world like the words of God.

November 1914

Translated from the German by Patrick Bridgwater.

AUGUST STRAMM

Guard-Duty

A star frightens the steeple cross
a horse gasps smoke
iron clanks drowsily
mists spread
fears
staring shivering
shivering
cajoling
whispering
You!

Translated from the German by Patrick Bridgwater.

Battlefield

Yielding clod lulls iron off to sleep
bloods clot the patches where they oozed
rusts crumble
fleshes slime
sucking lusts around decay.
Murder on murder
blinks
in childish eyes.

January 1915

Translated from the German by Michael Hamburger.

ALBERT EHRENSTEIN

The Poet and War

I sang the songs of red ripped-up vengeance,
And I sang the stillness of the lake with wooded bays,
But none came to join me,
Steep, lonely
As the cicada singing,
I sang my song for myself.
My footsteps fade already, slackening
In the sand of travail.
With weariness my eyes drop from me,
I am weary of comfortless fords,
Of crossing waters, girls and streets.
In the abyss I do not remember
The shield and the spear.
Round me the whispering birches,
Round me the wind's shadow.
I fall asleep to the sound of the harp
Of other men
For whom it joyfully spills.
I do not stir,
For every thought and deed
Darkens the purity of the world.
1917 : Die rote Zeit

Translated from the German by Christopher Middleton.

Nocturnal Landscape

A constellation like day; the horizon behind it by lights
    and flares fingered and shrouded,
That went and came, fell or stood, restless, phantom-
    like; and if it went, deep night fell,
And if it came, then somewhere a town lay, white,
    shifting furtive a forest was made and a vale
Full of sleep, with torrents and indeterminate things,
    with graves and churchtowers, smashed, with
    climbing mists, moist, big-clouded,
With huts, where sleepers lay, where a dream walked,
    full of fever, full of strangeness, full of animal
    splendour, where abruptly a screen
Of cloud split open; and behind it swelled an ocean of
    stars, a dominion of rockets, a light sprang from the
    ravine,
Terrible, roaring, rumble of wheels on roads, and a
    man stepped darkly into the dark, by a dreadful
    nightmare amazed,
Saw the flight of fires migrating, heard butchery below,
    saw behind the darkness the city that ceaselessly
    blazed,
Heard in earth's belly a rolling, ponderous, gigantic,
    primeval, heard traffic travelling the roads, into the
    void, into the widening night, into a storm, grim in
    the west. Frantic, the ear
With the front's countless hammers, with the riders
    who came, stamping, hurrying, with the riders who

rode away, to turn into shadows, melt into the night,
there to rot,
Death slaughters them, and they lie under weeds,
heavy, fossil, with hands full of spiders, mouths
scabbed red and brown,
Eyes full of uttermost sleep, the circlet of shadow
around their brows, blue, waxen, decaying in the
smoke of the night
Which sank down, threw shadows far, which spread its
vault from hill to hill, over forest and rottenness,
over brains full of dreams, over the hundred dead
none carried away,
Over the mass of fire, over laughter and madness, over
crosses in fields, over pain and despair, over rubble
and ash, over the river and the ruined town . . .

1920

Translated from the German by Christopher Middleton.

YVAN GOLL

From *Requiem for the Dead of Europe*

Recitative (I)

Let me lament the exodus of so many men from their
  time;
Let me lament the women whose warbling hearts now
  scream;
Every lament let me note and add to the list,
When young widows sit by lamplight mourning for
  husbands lost;
I hear the blonde-voiced children crying for God their
  father at bedtime;
On every mantelpiece stand photographs wreathed with
  ivy, smiling, true to the past;
At every window stand lonely girls whose burning eyes
  are bright with tears;
In every garden lilies are growing, as though there's a
  grave to prepare;
In every street the cars are moving more slowly, as
  though to a funeral;
In every city of every land you can hear the passing-
  bell;
In every heart there's a single plaint,
I hear it more clearly every day.

1917

Translated from the German by Patrick Bridgwater.

Recitative (*VIII*)

Like a grey wall around Europe
The long battle ran.
The never-ending battle, the bogged-down battle, the
softening-up battle,
The battle that was never the final battle.
Oh, the monotony of trench-warfare! Oh, trench-grave!
Oh, sleep of starvation!
The bridges built of corpses!
The roads surfaced with corpses!
The walls cemented with corpses!
For months on end the horizon stared mysteriously and
glassily like a dead man's eye.
For years on end the distance rang like the same old
passing-bell.
The days were as alike as a pair of graves.
Oh, you heroes!
Crawling out on wet nights, mewling in the bitter cold,
you from your all-electric cities!
The sentry swapped ten nights' sleep for one cigarette;
whole regiments gambled away eternity for ten yards
of wasteland.
Full-blooded curses spat into the starlit mire. Damp cellars
littered with tinny booty captured from the enemy.
Oh, you Greek dancers, dwarfed in lousy caverns!
Popping up like Indians in fancy-dress when the
drums sounded the attack:
Before sticking your bayonet into his groin, did not one
of you see the Christ-like look of his opponent, did
not one of you notice that the man over there had a
kingly heart full of love?
Did not one of you still believe in his own and
mankind's conscience?
You brothers, fellow-men! Oh, you heroes!
1917

Translated from the German by Patrick Bridgwater.

GUILLAUME APOLLINAIRE

Shadow

Here you are beside me again
Memories of my companions killed in the war
The olive-branch of time
Memories that make only a single memory
As a hundred skins make only a single coat
As these thousands of wounds make only a single
   newspaper article
Impalpable and dark presence who have assumed
The changing shape of my shadow
An Indian on the watch through all Eternity
Shadow you creep beside me
But you do not hear me any more
You will not know any more the divine poems I sing
But I hear you still and see you still
Destinies
Multiple shadow may the sun preserve you
You who love me so much that you will never leave me
And who dance in the sun without stirring the dust
Shadow ink of the sun
Signature of my light
Holder of sorrows
A god that condescends

Translated from the French by Christopher Middleton.

CHARLES VILDRAC

Relief

In our place
Fresh troops have come
Sent up the line
As bait for death
Met face to face.

We needed all night to make our escape,
All night and its darkness,
Sweating, frozen, to cross
The martyr forest and its swamp
That shrapnel scourged.

All night in which to crouch,
Then to run like the wind,
Each man picking his moment,
Trusting to nerve and instinct
And his star.

But beyond the last entanglement,
Out of it all, on the firm road,
Met together, with no delays,
In the glow of the first pipes lit,

Then, mates, O lucky winners,
Then what stumbling voluble joy!

That was the joy of shipwrecked men
With hands and knees upon the shore,
Who laugh with an agonized happiness
As they recover their treasure again;

All the treasure of the vast world,
And of memory unplumbed,
And of the thirst that can be quenched,
And even of the pain you feel
In the shoulders since all danger passed.

And the future! Ah, the future!
Now it is smiling, in the dawn:
A future of two long weeks ahead,
In a barn at Neuvilly.

Ah, the appletrees in blossom!
I'll put blossoms into my letters.
I'll go and read in the middle of a field.
I'll go and have a wash in the river.

The man who is marching in front of me
Whistles a song that his neighbour sings
A song that is far away from war:
I hum it too, and savour it.
Yet: to think of those killed yesterday!

But the man who has tripped
Between death's legs and then
Recovers himself and breathes again,
Can only laugh or only weep:
He has not the heart to mourn.

Today's first light makes all too drunk
The man who finds himself alive;
He is weak and is amazed
To be dawdling so along the road.

And if he dreams it is of the bliss
Of taking off his boots to sleep
In a barn at Neuvilly.

Translated from the French by Christopher Middleton.

RENÉ ARCOS

The Dead

In the wind that blows
The veils of widows
All float on one side

And the mingled tears
Of a thousand sorrows
In one stream glide.

Pressing each other close the dead
Who own no hatred and no flag,
Their hair veneered with clotted blood,
The dead are all on the same side.

In the one clay where endlessly
Beginnings blend with the world that dies
The brothered dead lain cheek to cheek
Today atone for the same defeat.

Divided sons, fight on, fight on,
You lacerate humanity
And tear the earth apart in vain,
The dead are all on the same side;

Under the earth no more than one,
One field, one single hope, abide,
As for the universe can only be
One combat and one victory.

Translated from the French by Christopher Middleton.

GIUSEPPE UNGARETTI

Vigil

A whole night long
crouched close
to one of our men
butchered
with his clenched
mouth
grinning at the full moon
with the congestion
of his hands
thrust right
into my silence
I've written
letters filled with love

I have never been
so
coupled to life
Cima Quattro, 23 December 1915

Translated from the Italian by Jonathan Griffin.

Brothers

What regiment d'you belong to
brothers?

Word shaking
in the night

Leaf barely born

In the simmering air
involuntary revolt
of the man present at his
brittleness

Brothers
Mariano, 11 July 1916

Translated from the Italian by Jonathan Griffin.

Rivers

This mutilated tree gives
Me support, left in this pot-hole.
It has the bitterness of a circus
Before or after the show.
I watch
The quiet passage of
Clouds over the moon.

This morning I stretched
Myself in an urn of water,
Like a relic, and rested.

The Isonzo scoured
Me like
One of its stones.

I pulled my four
Limbs together,
And went, like an acrobat,
Over the water.

Crouched by my clothes
Fouled with war, I inclined
My head, like a Bedouin,
To receive the sun.

This is the Isonzo.
And it is there I
Most see myself
In the universe
A compliant
Thread.

My pain is
When I do not believe
Myself in harmony.

But those hidden
Hands give as they knead me
A rare joy.

I have relived
The stages of my life.

The Serchio: from
Which have drawn, perhaps
For two thousand years
My country people, my father,
My mother.

This is the Nile
That has seen me be born,
And grow
And burn in ignorance on
Extending plains.

This is the Seine; and I mingled
In that muddiness learning each
Part of all myself.

These are my rivers confluent
In the Isonzo.

This is my nostalgia
That in each
One shines through me, now
It is night, and my life seems
A budding
Off of shades.

Translated from the Italian by Jon Silkin.

No More Crying Out

Cease murdering the dead.
If you hope not to perish, if you
Want sound of them again,
Stop crying out, cease
The crying out of it.

They have a barely heard whispering,
No more than the increase of grass,
Happy where no man passes.

Translated from the Italian by Jon Silkin.

The Drum by John Scott (1730–83)

I hate that drum's discordant sound,
Parading round, and round, and round:
To thoughtless youth it pleasure yields,
And lures from cities and from fields,
To sell their liberty for charms
Of tawdry lace, and glittering arms;
And when Ambition's voice commands,
To march, and fight, and fall, in foreign lands.

I hate that drum's discordant sound,
Parading round, and round, and round:
To me it talks of ravag'd plains,
And burning towns, and ruin'd swains,
And mangled limbs, and dying groans,
And widows' tears, and orphans' moans;
And all that Misery's hand bestows,
To fill the catalogue of human woes.

BIBLIOGRAPHY

ALDINGTON, RICHARD, *Death of a Hero*, Chatto & Windus, 1929; *The Complete Poems*, Allan Wingate, 1948.

ARNOLD, MATTHEW, *Poems*, O.U.P., 1926.

BARBUSSE, HENRI, *Under Fire* (trans. W. Fitzwater Wray), Dent, 1926.

BERGONZI, BERNARD, *Heroes' Twilight*, Constable, 1965.

BERRY, FRANCIS, *Herbert Read*, British Council Monograph, 1961.

BLUNDEN, EDMUND, *Poems 1914–1930*, Cobden-Sanderson, 1930; *Undertones of War*, Penguin, 1937.

BRIDGWATER, PATRICK (trans. and ed.), 'German Poems of the 1914–18 War', *The Journals of Pierre Menard*, no. 3, July, 1969; 'German Poetry and the First World War', *European Studies Review*, I, no. 2, 1971.

BROOKE, RUPERT, *Poetical Works*, Faber & Faber, 1946.

BYRON, LORD, *Don Juan, The Poetical Works*, O.U.P., 1909.

COHEN, JOSEPH, 'The Three Roles of Siegfried Sassoon', *Tulane Studies of English*, VI, 1956; *Journey to the Trenches/ The Life of Isaac Rosenberg*, Robson Books, 1975.

COLERIDGE, SAMUEL TAYLOR, 'Fears in Solitude', *The Poems*, Edward Moxon, 1856; *Biographia Literaria*, Dent, 1956.

COOKE, WILLIAM, *Edward Thomas/A Critical Biography*, Faber & Faber, 1970; 'The War Diary of Edward Thomas', *Stand*, vol. 19, no. 4, 1978.

COOMBES, H., *Edward Thomas*, Chatto & Windus, 1956.

CUMMINGS, E. E., *The Enormous Room*, Boni & Liveright, 1922; *Complete Poems*, MacGibbon & Kee, 1968.

DEPPE, W. G., MIDDLETON, CHRISTOPHER, and SCHÖN-
HERR, HERBERT, *Ohne Hass Und Fahne* (*No Hatred and No
Flag*), Rowolt, Hamburg, 1959.

FARJEON, ELEANOR, *Edward Thomas/The Last Four Years*,
Bodley Head, 1958.

FLINT, F. S., *Otherworld/Cadences*, Poetry Bookshop, 1920.

FORD, FORD MADOX, *On Heaven/and Other Poems*, Poetry
Bookshop, 1918; *Parades End*, Bodley Head, 1963.

FORSTER, E. M., *Howards End*, E. Arnold, 1910.

FUSSELL, PAUL, *The Great War and Modern Memory*, O.U.P.,
1975.

GARDNER, BRIAN (ed.), *Up the Line to Death*, Methuen,
1964.

GRAVES, ROBERT, *The Poems*, Doubleday Anchor, New York,
1958; *Goodbye to All That*, Penguin Books, 1960.

GRUBB, FREDERICK, *A Vision of Reality*, Chatto & Windus,
1965.

GURNEY, IVOR, *Severn and the Somme*, Sidgwick & Jackson,
1917; *War's Embers*, Sidgwick & Jackson, 1919; *Poems*,
Hutchinson, 1954; *Poems of Ivor Gurney 1890–1937*, Chatto
& Windus, 1973.

HAMBURGER, MICHAEL, and MIDDLETON, CHRISTOPHER,
'No Hatred and No Flag', *Encounter*, no. 85, 1960; *Modern
German Poetry 1910–1960*, MacGibbon & Kee, 1963.

HARDING, DENYS, *Experience Into Words*, Chatto & Windus,
1970.

HARDY, THOMAS, *The Dynasts*, Macmillan, 1930; *The Collected
Poems*, Macmillan, 1952.

HASEK, JAROSLAV, *The Good Soldier Svejk*, (trans. Cecil
Parrott), Penguin Books in association with William Heine-
mann, 1973.

HENRYSON, ROBERT, *Testament of Cresseid/Poems*, Clarendon
Press, 1963.

HIBBERD, DOMINIC (ed.), *Wilfred Owen/War Poems and
Others*, Chatto & Windus, 1973; 'Images of Darkness in
the Poems of Wilfred Owen', *Durham University Journal*,
March 1974; 'Wilfred Owen', British Council Monograph,
1974.

HURD, MICHAEL, *The Ordeal of Ivor Gurney*, O.U.P., 1978.

JOHNSTON, JOHN H., *English Poetry of the First World War*, O.U.P., 1964; 'The Heroic Vision', *Review of Politics*, 24 January 1968.

JONES, A. R., *The Life and Opinions of Thomas Ernest Hulme*, Gollancz, 1960.

JONES, DAVID, *Epoch and Artist*, Faber & Faber, 1959; *In Parenthesis*, Faber & Faber, 1963.

JONES, PETER (ed.), *Imagist Poetry*, Penguin Books, 1972.

KIPLING, RUDYARD, *Verse*, Hodder & Stoughton, 1940.

KYLE, GALLOWAY (ed.), *Soldier Poets/Songs of the Fighting Men*, Erskine MacDonald, 1916.

LARKIN, PHILIP (ed.), *The Oxford Book of Twentieth Century Verse*, O.U.P., 1973.

LAWRENCE, D. H., *Collected Poems*, Martin Secker, 1928.

LEAVIS, F. R., *New Bearings in English Poetry*, Chatto & Windus, 1950; *Thought, Words and Creativity*, Chatto & Windus, 1976.

LIDDIARD, JEAN, *Isaac Rosenberg/The Half Used Life*, Victor Gollancz, 1975.

LIEBKNECHT, KARL L., *The Future Belongs to the People*, Macmillan (New York), 1918.

LLOYD, BERTRAM (ed.), *Poems Written During the Great War 1914–1918*, Allen & Unwin, 1918.

MANNING, FREDERIC, *Eidolon*, Murray, 1917; *Her Privates We*, Peter Davis, 1964.

MARSH, EDWARD (ed.), *Georgian Poetry* (5 vols.), The Poetry Bookshop, 1911–22.

MATTHEWS, GEOFFREY, 'Brooke and Owen', *Stand*, vol. 4, no. 3, 1960.

MONRO, HAROLD, *Collected Poems*, Cobden-Sanderson, 1933.

MONTAGUE, C. E., *Disenchantment*, Chatto & Windus, 1922.

NICHOLS, ROBERT, *Ardours and Endurances*, Chatto & Windus, 1918.

OWEN, HAROLD, *Journey from Obscurity/Wilfred Owen* (III. War), O.U.P., 1965.

OWEN, WILFRED, *The Collected Poems*, Chatto & Windus, 1963; *Letters*, O.U.P., 1967; *War Poems and Others*, Chatto & Windus, 1973.

PARSONS, IAN, *Men Who March Away*, Chatto & Windus, 1965.

POUND, EZRA, *Personae/Collected Shorter Poems*, Faber & Faber, 1952.

READ, HERBERT, *The Contrary Experience*, Faber & Faber, 1963; *Collected Poems*, Faber & Faber, 1966.

REMARQUE, ERICH MARIA, *All Quiet on the Western Front* (trans. A. W. Wheen), Putnam, 1954.

RICHARDS, FRANK, *Old Soldiers Never Die*, with an introduction by Robert Graves, Faber & Faber, 1964.

RICKWORD, EDGELL, *Behind the Eyes/Collected Poems and Selected Translations*, Carcanet New Press, 1976.

ROSENBERG, ISAAC, *The Complete Works*, Chatto & Windus, 1937; *The Collected Works*, Chatto & Windus, 1979.

SASSOON, SIEGFRIED, *The Complete Memoirs of George Sherston*, Faber & Faber, 1937; *Siegfried's Journey*, Faber & Faber, 1945; *Collected Poems*, Faber & Faber, 1947.

SCANNELL, VERNON, *Edward Thomas*, British Council Monograph, 1965.

SHELLEY, PERCY BYSSHE, *The Revolt of Islam/The Poetical Works*, O.U.P., 1909.

SILKIN, JON, *Out of Battle*, O.U.P., 1972.

SORLEY, CHARLES HAMILTON, *The Letters*, C.U.P., 1919; *Marlborough and Other Poems*, C.U.P., 1932.

STALLWORTHY, JON, *Wilfred Owen/A Biography*, O.U.P. and Chatto & Windus, 1974.

STEAD, C. K., *The New Poetic*, Hutchinson, 1964.

SYMONS, JULIAN (ed.), *An Anthology of War Poetry*, Pelican Books, 1942.

THOMAS, EDWARD, *Collected Poems*, Faber & Faber, 1936; 'The Diary of Edward Thomas', *Anglo-Welsh Review*, vol. 20, no. 45, 1971; *Collected Poems*, Collins, 1973.

THOMAS, HELEN, *As it was . . . World without End*, Heinemann, 1935.

THORPE, MICHAEL, *Siegfried Sassoon*, O.U.P., 1966.

TRAKL, GEORG, *Decline* (trans. Michael Hamburger), The Latin Press, 1952; *Twenty Poems of Georg Trakl* (trans. James Wright and Robert Bly), The Sixties Press, 1961.

TROTSKY, LEON, *Literature and Revolution* (trans. Rose Strunsky), Ann Arbor, 1960.

UNGARETTI, GIUSEPPE, *Selected Poems* (trans. Patrick Creagh), Penguin Books, 1971.

WEIL, SIMONE, 'The Iliad, a poem of force' (trans. Mary McCarthy), *Politics*, Politics Publishing Company, 1945.

WELLAND, D. S. R., *Wilfred Owen/A Critical Study*, Chatto & Windus, 1960.

WILLEY, BASIL, *Samuel Taylor Coleridge*, Chatto & Windus, 1972.

WILSON, JEAN MOORCRAFT, *Isaac Rosenberg/Poet and Painter*, Cecil Woolf, 1975.

WORDSWORTH, WILLIAM, *Lyrical Ballads*, Methuen, 1960; *The Prelude*, Penguin Books, 1971.

YEATS, W. B. (ed.), *The Oxford Book of Modern Verse*, O.U.P., 1936.

INDEX OF POETS AND TRANSLATORS

INDEX OF FIRST LINES

INDEX OF TITLES

Indexes compiled by Neil Astley.

MORE ABOUT PENGUINS
AND PELICANS

For further information about books available from Penguins
please write to Dept EP, Penguin Books Ltd, Harmondsworth,
Middlesex UB7 0DA.

In the U.S.A.: For a complete list of books available from Penguins in
the United States write to Dept CS, Penguin Books, 625 Madison
Avenue, New York, New York 10022.

In Canada: For a complete list of books available from Penguins in
Canada write to Penguin Books Canada Ltd, 2801 John Street,
Markham, Ontario L3R 1B4.

In Australia: For a complete list of books available from Penguins in
Australia write to the Marketing Department, Penguin Books Australia
Ltd, P.O. Box 257, Ringwood, Victoria 3134.

'Lest we forget'

PENGUIN BOOKS ON THE FIRST WORLD WAR

IN FLANDERS FIELDS
Leon Wolff

Passchendaele 1917. There is no name more evocative of the 'mud and blood' of the gallant and inglorious trench warfare on the Western Front. Leon Wolff's classic account of the Flanders campaign was described by Major-General J.F.C. Fuller as 'an outstanding book . . . much more than a military history, rather an invocation which summons from out of the depths of the past the catastrophic year of 1917 . . . Here is brought to light again all its many facets, its antagonisms, its blunders, its horrors and its heroism'.

THE PRICE OF GLORY: Verdun 1916
Alistair Horne

'Brilliantly written . . . almost like a historical novel – except that it is true' – Field Marshal Viscount Montgomery

Verdun was the battle that lasted ten months; the battle where at least 700,000 men died, along a front of fifteen miles; the battle which aimed less to defeat the enemy than to bleed him to death; the battle whose once fertile terrain is even now 'the nearest thing to desert in Europe'. Alistair Horne's profoundly moving study shows it to be also the key to an understanding of the First World War.

GOODBYE TO ALL THAT
Robert Graves

Robert Graves' autobiography first appeared in 1929.

'It is a permanently valuable work of literary art, and indispensable for the historian either of the First World War or of modern English poetry . . . Apart, however, from its exceptional value as a war document, this book has also the interest of being one of the most candid self-portraits of a poet, warts and all, ever painted. The sketches of friends of Mr Graves, like T.E. Lawrence, are beautifully vivid' – *The Times Literary Supplement*

SAGITTARIUS RISING
Cecil Lewis

'Did I dive headlong, guns stuttering, into the Richthofen Circus that night Ball was killed? Did I range over darkened London, nervous under the antennae of her searchlights, hunting for Gothas?'

This reminiscent epic of adventurous youth conveys vividly the thrills of flight in those flimsy machines, the hazards, the courtesies, and the mortal dangers of war in the air. When it was first published in 1936, Bernard Shaw wrote: 'This is a book which everybody should read. It is the autobiography of an ace, and no common ace either.'

THE SPANISH FARM TRILOGY
R.H. Mottram

As the line of the Western Front ebbs and flows across Flanders, the Spanish Farm – built to withstand the wars of an earlier century – faces this one with the same imperturbable stolidity. And to the men who come to know the farm, the rough comfort of its buildings, Jerome Vanderlynden's persistent preoccupation with his crops, and his daughter Madeleine's bourgeois practicality offer an oasis of enduring sanity to which they turn with relief.

The Spanish Farm, Sixty-Four, Ninety-Four and *The Crime at Vanderlynden's* were first published as a trilogy in 1927, when *The Times Literary Supplement* acclaimed it as 'perhaps the most significant work of its kind in English that the War has yet occasioned'.

THE WARS
Timothy Findley

Winner of Canada's Governor-General Award and of the City of Toronto Book Award

A book about war that illuminates all wars. A book with the immediacy – and impact – of a film. The true story of a young Canadian officer in 1915, drawn into the most traumatic war of all time.

'It is a book that demands superlatives and that stands comparison with any fiction being produced in the English language. I doubt if any reader will think that statement too sweeping' – *Toronto Star*

THE FIRST WORLD WAR

A. J. P. Taylor

AN ILLUSTRATED HISTORY

For four years, while statesmen and generals blundered, the massed armies of Europe writhed in a festival of mud and blood. All the madness, massacres and mutinies of the foulest war in history are brought home here by action pictures of the day and the text of an uncompromising historian.

THE SHIP THAT HUNTED ITSELF

Colin Simpson

At the beginning of World War I, the captains of British ocean liner *Carmania* and German liner *Cap Trafalgar* were ordered to convert their ships into armed merchant cruisers. Neither was particularly strong, so both resorted to disguise.

By coincidence, each disguised herself as the other. By an even greater coincidence, they met in the south Atlantic – and fought one of the most curious and heroic engagements in naval history.

THE FACE OF BATTLE

A STUDY OF AGINCOURT, WATERLOO AND THE SOMME

John Keegan

'A brilliant achievement . . . In this book, which is so creative, so original, one learns as much about the nature of man as of battle' – J.H. Plumb in the *New York Times Book Review*

The Face of Battle is military history from the battlefield: a look at the direct experience of individuals at the 'point of maximum danger'. Without the myth-making elements of rhetoric and xenophobia, breaking away from the stylized format of battle descriptions, John Keegan has written probably the definitive model for military historians. In his scrupulous reassessment of three battles, he manages to convey their reality, and their significance for the participants, whether facing the arrow cloud of Agincourt in 1415 or the steel rain of the Somme in 1916.

THE RIDDLE OF THE SANDS
Erskine Childers

The Riddle of the Sands is regarded by many critics as one of the best spy stories ever written; certainly, it was the first modern espionage story and remains a classic of the genre.

Its unique flavour comes from its richly detailed technical background of inshore sailing in the Baltic and North Seas, from its remarkable air of authenticity, and its evocation of the world of the late 1890s – an atmosphere of suspicion and intrigue that was soon to lead to war.

THE AFRICAN QUEEN
C.S. Forester

A crazy, breathless, steam-powered adventure of the First World War.

C.S. Forester is at his most entertaining in this story of the missionary woman and the Cockney mechanic marooned in German Central Africa. As they fight their ramshackle old launch down-river 'to strike a blow for England', the 'African Queen' seems to breathe the spirit of Hornblower himself.

GREENMANTLE
John Buchan

For England and her allies 1915 was a crisis point in the First World War. In the East a new prophet has been promised, and the fanatical spirit of Islam threatens to harness itself to the might of the German war machine.

In pursuit of the mysterious and elusive 'Greenmantle', Richard Hannay is despatched on an undercover mission through occupied Europe to Constantinople. It is a mission that will demand all his courage and resourcefulness.